Introduction

This block introduces the importance of markets as a requirement for successful innovation. The main aim of this block is to consider how innovative products can be designed to meet the needs of potential users and purchasers. In your study of this block you will be introduced to some of the concepts and techniques used by marketing departments. This will help you to understand how companies view and research markets.

You will then look at ways product designers themselves carry out research into the needs and wishes of the people they are designing for, to create appropriate and attractive products.

An understanding of markets demands consideration of the contexts for those markets. The later sections of the block briefly look at contextual topics such as psychology, culture and globalisation.

Aims and learning outcomes

Aims

- To develop an understanding of the importance of markets in the development and diffusion of products.

- To know how information about users is gathered and brought into the design process.

Learning outcomes

After studying this block, you should have achieved the following learning outcomes.

1   Knowledge and understanding

You should understand:

1.1   How design and markets have evolved.

1.2   The elements necessary for a market to exist.

1.3   The different approaches to marketing that are adopted by companies.

1.4   The ways in which market sectors are segmented.

1.5   The relationships that exist between manufacturers and purchasers.

1.6   The importance of brands.

1.7   The distinction between the market research and sales aspects of marketing.

1.8   Factors that make up the market environment.

1.9   Techniques that are used for market research and their usefulness.

1.10 The value of user-centred design as a way of creating successful products.

1.11 The role of testing houses in the design process.

1.12 The importance of psychology and culture as influences on purchasing decisions.

1.13 The influences on organisational purchasing.

1.14 The issues raised by globalisation of markets.

2   Cognitive skills

You should be able to:

2.1   Explain terms such as markets and marketing, saturation and diffusion and give appropriate examples.

2.2   Explain market sectors and segmentation, giving appropriate examples.

2.3   Explain what is meant by a market decision support system.

2.4   Identify the trends on which companies collect market information.

The Open University

Block 2
Markets:
designing for people

Georgy Holden

T307 Innovation: designing for a sustainable future

This publication forms part of an Open University course T307 *Innovation: designing for a sustainable future*. Details of this and other Open University courses can be obtained from the Student Registration and Enquiry Service, The Open University, PO Box 197, Milton Keynes, MK7 6BJ, United Kingdom: tel. +44 (0)870 300 60 90, email general-enquiries@open.ac.uk

Alternatively, you may visit the Open University website at http://www.open.ac.uk where you can learn more about the wide range of courses and packs offered at all levels by The Open University.

To purchase a selection of Open University course materials visit http://www.ouw.co.uk, or contact Open University Worldwide, Walton Hall, Milton Keynes MK7 6AA, United Kingdom for a brochure. tel. +44 (0)1908 858793; fax +44 (0)1908 858787; email ouw-customer-services@open.ac.uk

The Open University
Walton Hall, Milton Keynes
MK7 6AA

First published 2006. Second edition 2010.

Edited, designed and typeset by the Open University.

Printed and bound in the United Kingdom by Martins the Printers Ltd.

ISBN 978 1 8487 3051 9

2.1

Contents

2.5 Explain the difference between qualitative and quantitative market research.

2.6 Identify the main steps in market research.

2.7 Explain standards and standardisation in terms of markets.

2.8 Explain what is meant by the marketing mix and identify the different elements, using appropriate examples.

2.9 Explain the product life cycle, giving examples.

2.10 Identify pricing strategies.

2.11 Explain the total product concept.

2.12 Identify product performance in terms of market growth and market share.

3   Key skills

You should be able to:

3.1 Develop your skills in information literacy through devising and conducting research.

3.2 Develop your communication skills by evaluating and synthesising information from different sources.

4   Practical and professional skills

You should be able to use some of the user-centred research techniques in your own project work.

1 Making products that sell

1.1 Selling ideas to people

There seems to be no limit to human creativity and ingenuity, and the increasing rate of technological change over the past century shows how ideas build on one another until completely new ideas emerge. However ideas alone are not enough. The crucial ingredient that turns an invention into an innovation is the launch of the invention onto the marketplace. Inventive ideas have to be developed and embodied as designs, and these designs have to be offered for sale. There may be many measures of the success of an innovation, for example influence on future product development, technical superiority and acclaim from other designers. However the bottom line is that those innovations that are seen as the most successful are those that sell.

In this block I will be looking at some of the factors that lead to successful innovations and how designers can find out the information they need to help their innovative products to meet the needs, wants and desires of those who will ultimately buy and use them. The examples that you will see here vary – some are incremental innovations to products that are evolving gradually, others are more radical and fundamental innovations. Wherever a product sits on the spectrum of innovation markets are important. However the techniques used to find out about relevant markets and create sales strategies will differ depending on whether the product is familiar to potential purchasers or users.

In the past the concerns of users were often seen simply as marketing issues and met either by some retrospective adjustment to the product once it had been designed or by advertising campaigns to persuade the user of the wisdom of their choice. However recent years have seen a changing emphasis towards a consideration of user needs at the earliest conceptual design stages of product development. There is sound economic sense in this approach. For a product to be successful, people must want to buy it. Finding out who those people might be, what they like and giving them a voice in the development can lead to products that both please the purchasers and sell well.

Some of the examples that you will encounter in this block are incremental innovations – products that have evolved bit by bit. Other examples are of more radical and fundamental innovation but for products of all kinds, whether incremental or radical innovations, markets are important.

1.2 People and markets

Companies often talk about markets, but what do they mean? The term market, like the word design, can be used in a number of different ways. The term market can be used to mean people, physical spaces, the action of buying or selling, and the rate of sale. The only way to know which of these is being referred to is by the context of the discussion.

There are some common elements though that are found in the various definitions of market (Figures 1–3). These elements include people, goods or services, and the exchange of money. Of these, the most important to hold in mind when developing a new product is people. If you design something, whether it is a new can opener or a production plant for an industrial process, at the end of the development process you need people to buy it.

Figure 1   Markets were originally places where people came together to trade food they had grown and objects they had made

Figure 2   Many supermarkets now sell a wide range of consumer goods imported from all over the world Source: Chetwood Associates

This Sainsbury supermarket in Greenwich, London is not an ordinary store. It incorporates a photovoltaic roof and wind turbines. It consumes half the energy of comparable stores.

But the other elements are important too. The challenge for any company working on innovations is to balance the market elements to create a product or service that people want, at a price they are willing to pay. The relative importance of these elements will vary depending on the nature of the product, but to concentrate solely on one of these elements and neglect the others would almost inevitably lead to failure.

Figure 3 In the 1990s the internet became a market. Entertainment products, such as books, CDs, DVDs and computer games, were easy and often cheaper to buy in this way Source: Amazon.co.uk

Later on in this block I will be looking at what is known in marketing jargon as the *marketing mix*, which means the balance of factors that affect the success or failure of a product. For now it is sufficient to understand that the success of any product hinges on how that product is perceived by those who will purchase it. There is a whole marketing industry whose job it is to find the correct balance of elements to make potential purchasers perceive new products in a favourable light.

Exercise 1   Why did you buy it?

Think briefly about your own purchasing behaviour. Have you bought a new product recently? Was the product a replacement for something you already had or something completely new to you? What influenced your purchasing decision? Where did you buy the product?

Spend 10 minutes on this before looking at my comments below.

Discussion

Obviously I do not know what you bought but it might have been a mobile phone, television or DVD player. These are all items that have huge markets and are widely available. Did anything influence your purchase, for example advertising, a newspaper, magazine or internet article or the recommendation of a friend? Did you carefully research alternative products, weighing up features, shape and size, and prices to decide on the one to buy or did you buy on impulse because a product you intended to buy happened to be on sale for a good price at the supermarket? Perhaps you are an internet shopper who searches online for the best deal.

Alternatively, you may be someone who always buys from the same shop because the sales staff gives you good advice, or do you always buy a particular brand because you trust it? If the product you bought was a replacement for something you already owned, your purchase might have been influenced by your previous experience of the product. You may, for example, always buy the same make of car, mobile phone or computer because you know the brand and feel happy with it.

You may be someone who carefully considers environmental aspects, such as energy-use or materials, and you seek out so-called green products. Or perhaps you had to make your decision based on cost or available space, which meant finding a compromise that fitted your constraints.

It is possible that you recognise more than one of the purchasing behaviours described above and that you use different behaviours at different times, for different sorts of purchases. For example you may shop around on the internet for the best-priced software or books but always buy your white goods from a store that offers reliable service. Most people will look for more information and take longer to make decisions about expensive purchases, such as cars and central heating systems, than they do for cheaper products and consumable items.

1.3 Relationship between maker and user

Marketing is essentially about the relationships that exist between manufacturers, distributors, retailers and purchasers. These relationships are not static – they change and develop over time and are affected by such factors as:

- the nature of the product

- the maturity of the industry

- the size, nature and affluence of markets sought

- the level of industrialisation in the manufacturing and purchasing countries.

There are two aspects to marketing. The first, the *market research* aspect, is concerned with identifying the needs of potential markets to inform new product development. The second, the *sales and marketing* aspect, is concerned with selling products, new and old.

In the past within manufacturing companies the relationship between manufacturer and purchaser was usually the concern of marketing departments. These departments are still important as the shapers and movers of companies' relationships with their customers.

However these relationships are now more complex than they were in the early days of mass production. In consumer and commercial markets few manufacturers sell direct to their end-users anymore. Yet increasingly, product designers are also concerned with these relationships as the process of product design becomes more *people-centred*. You will learn more about how these concerns are brought into the design process in Section 4.

A strong relationship between manufacturer and purchaser is most likely to result in an innovation becoming a widely used, diffused product. It is therefore important for manufacturers to build and strengthen this relationship in whatever ways they can. This ranges from ensuring that products meet purchasers' needs and aspirations through to aggressive advertising to convince purchasers of the advantages of their products relative to the competition.

1.3.1 A short history of marketing

In the past 100 years the business philosophies that underpin the relationship between manufacturers and purchasers have developed and changed. This has brought about new ways of thinking about products and reconsidering how they can be sold. A summary of these philosophies follows.

Late nineteenth to early twentieth century – production orientation or 'sell what you can make'

In the early part of the twentieth century, demand for products exceeded the amount that could be supplied. Manufacturers were concerned with developing their production plants in such a way as to produce items cheaply enough to sell in quantity. They focused the efforts of the company towards production. Production-orientated companies 'sell what they can make'. Product development in production-orientated companies is driven by production considerations, for example the sorts of machinery, processes and working practices within the company. The epitome of this view is that of Henry Ford, who is reputed to have said that buyers could have his Model T Ford in any colour, as long as it was black.

One reason that companies adopted a production-orientated approach was the cost of tooling up for the production of a new product. This was a major constraint to innovation in the past. In the last two decades of the twentieth century the introduction of computer-controlled machinery and new production processes gave companies a greater degree of flexibility and in some instances reduced the cost of changes to products, allowing a move away from production orientation toward a more marketing-orientated view.

1920s to 1950s – sales orientation or 'make what you can sell'

Sales- and marketing-orientated companies make what they can sell. With the development of production processes that enabled companies to make large quantities of goods with ease, companies' orientation shifted to sales. The new philosophy was to persuade people to buy the goods that were being turned out. The marketing organisation identified potential customers and developed sales strategies such as advertising to convince those customers the product met their needs.

Customer responses to sales strategies were monitored closely. In such an organisation the marketing manager would look at proposed new products and consider which customers the product might be aimed at. Sales-orientated companies were concerned to compete with their rivals by making their product appear more attractive to consumers through their advertising and sales strategies.

After the 1950s – product orientation or 'make the product do more'

As expectations developed, and affluence spread, the emphasis of many manufacturers moved onto the product itself and its functions, developing more features as a way of making products more attractive. The product became the main orientation of the company.

Looking, for example, at the development of a product such as the vacuum cleaner, these marketing philosophies can be seen in action. When this innovation was first launched, manufacturers such as Hoover concentrated on developing the production facilities to enable the vacuum cleaner to be made in quantity. Once this was possible, a more sales-orientated approach was adopted and teams of salespeople went knocking on doors trying to interest householders in purchasing these new cleaners, and advertisements were placed in newspapers and magazines.

As the uptake of vacuum cleaners became widespread, competing manufacturers looked at ways to improve and differentiate their products, such as adding cleaning attachments, easy to change dust bags and a blow function.

1.3.2 Recent marketing philosophies

All of the philosophies discussed above can still be found, and are certainly present in some developing and newly industrialised countries. However in the sophisticated marketplace of the industrialised world, new philosophies have emerged that are now influencing company strategies.

Consumer orientation or 'find out what people want'

This philosophy puts consumer wants, needs and desires at the centre of all of a company's activities. Consumer needs are considered from the start of the design process. This is quite different to the sales-orientated approach, in which a product proposal is made and then possible markets are considered.

The consumer-orientated view takes the potential user as the starting point for generating design ideas and follows through with consideration of the potential customer at every stage of product development, through to aftersales service. This philosophy requires the willingness of the individual staff members who make up the company to be customer focused.

Relationship marketing or 'customers are for life'

This approach to the marketing relationship emphasises the importance of building a relationship with customers in the long term. This approach will consider ways the different products of a company might meet the needs of its customers throughout the customers' lives. This shapes and informs the range of products offered. For example an audio equipment manufacturer may make a range of CD players, ranging from one designed for children through to players for teenagers, young adults and mature adults.

The financial value of customer loyalty to a particular *brand* can be immense if that customer remains loyal throughout their lifetime. Throughout this block you will find examples of products, many of which you will recognise. Your feelings about those products, and whether they are products that you would wish to own, will be strongly coloured by your perception of the manufacturers' brand.

Societal and ethical marketing or 'attracting the ethical consumer'

A growing number of companies are now putting an emphasis on concern for social responsibility. Such companies consider the impact of their activities on society and on the environment. Although, in this approach, the company concerns go beyond the customers' wants and needs, customers are often attracted to these companies' products because this ethical approach adds a feel-good factor to their purchasing behaviour.

An awareness of all these marketing trends is important because it offers some important pointers to any would-be innovator. The pointers are these:

- think about user needs

- think about how a product sits in a product range and factors that add value to achieve brand loyalty

- think about ethical issues such as social and environmental impact.

Some examples of recent marketing philosophies are shown in Figure 4.

Consumer orientation This mp3 player was developed as a collaboration between Philips and the sports clothing manufacturer Nike. As a result of extensive consumer research the player clips to sportswear and has light, flexible leads and headphones that will not impede anyone wearing them and running.	
Relationship marketing An example of relationship marketing in the retail sector is the customer loyalty card that is used by supermarkets to encourage repeat custom. Such schemes have dual purpose giving the retailer information about the buying habits of their customers, which influences the products that are offered. The range of sports shoe manufacturer Nike starts with this tiny trainer for babies as a way of building relationship with the brand.	
Societal marketing This laundry detergent uses its brand name as well as the information on the box to convey the message about the use of environmentally friendly ingredients. The box contains a cleverly designed cardboard scoop that can be recycled after use. The Body Shop is a successful toiletries and cosmetics retailer that has made a virtue of the company's commitment to animal-free testing and more recently goods accepted by the standard-setting and certification organisation Fairtrade.	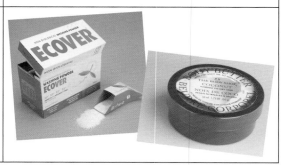

Figure 4   Contemporary marketing philosophies Source: Philips

Exercise 2   Identify marketing philosophies

Look around you at products, their packaging and the related advertising materials. Can you find any examples of the three kinds of recent marketing philosophies above?

Discussion

There are many examples of products with these different philosophies. There is less of the societal approach to marketing on display relative to the other two approaches, but a trip to the supermarket will find fair trade and organic goods that exemplify this.

Relationship marketing is often found with well-established brand names, such as car manufacturers who make a range of cars to meet different life stages.

Consumer-orientated marketing is exemplified by lots of products, for example products for personal use and grooming such as music players, beauty appliances and shavers.

1.4 Market research and sales

As you have been reading about the different relationships between companies and markets, you may have noticed there are two aspects to these relationships. On the one hand is the need to find out about possible markets, which is *market research*, and on the other hand is the buying and selling relationship, which is the *sales and marketing strategy*.

Both aspects are important to the successful creation and subsequent diffusion of new products. These two aspects often influence each other. Information that is gathered from market research is used to create sales and marketing strategies that will persuade potential purchasers to choose the product. Conversely, sales and marketing strategies may influence future market research by changing purchasers' perceptions of products.

1.5 Importance of markets

It has already been stated that when people talk about the success of a new product or innovation they are usually talking about how well it has sold. There are of course other measures of success, such as how well a product performs the function for which it has been designed, whether it receives critical acclaim from experts and so on. However at the end of the day, companies will measure success in terms of volume of sales and the amount of profit made.

This means the market is a key factor in the process of innovation. Without a potential market, products are doomed to fail, although the existence of a market does not automatically ensure success for a product.

Companies need to consider markets at three levels of their activity:

- *Strategic plan*. At this level the company decides what its main business will be in the long term. This entails planning the products to be produced and sold, the markets to be targeted and the distribution channels for products.

- *New product development*. At this level the company concentrates on specific products, having identified customer needs and wishes. It considers how customer needs can be embodied in those new products. The identification of needs may be done through market or user research.

- *Sales and marketing strategy*. When markets are identified, decisions have to be made about how products are to be sold within an overall strategy. Attention must be paid to the launch and selling of a product, and to the design of packaging and advertisements.

1.5.1 Strategic planning

The strategic planning carried out by a company will inform and influence all of the company's product development activities and set the overall context in which new products will be created and disseminated. However throughout the design process the company will also be concerned with market information at a more specific and detailed level. For example at the start of the process an idea for a product may come about through market or user research.

As you will see in later sections, such research may also influence the design and development stages of the product. In the company Philips Design, the strategic design group have run a number of projects looking at design for the future. One of a number of products that have come out of the research into computers integrated into home appliances – labelled ambient intelligence – is the iPronto, which uses computing technology to enable users to control all the appliances in their homes (Figure 5). The iPronto also includes such facilities as a permanent, wireless internet connection, and will download program information and display pictures stored on the home computer.

Figure 5   Philips iPronto super-remote controller contains an extensive database of manufacturers' infrared codes, making it simple to use Source: Philips Electronics UK Ltd

1.5.2 New product development

All large companies, most medium-sized companies and some small companies have dedicated marketing departments. In addition companies sometimes employ marketing agencies to carry out specific pieces of market research. However in some cutting-edge companies, designers are doing their own market research. The focus of designer-led research into the market is, inevitably, the potential user.

Marketing professionals still devise and conduct research that gives the company a good overview of potential markets and possibilities. Designers then take this market research as a starting point and look for ways to turn this general data into information that puts names, faces and personal information to the potential users, making the process of product development more intimate and personal than it would otherwise be. You will learn more about this in Section 4.

In 2002–2003 the Singapore government, in conjunction with several consortia of companies, ran five projects to look at aspects of the connected home. The connected home is a recent concept where information and communication technologies are fully integrated into day-to-day living. One of these projects called Unihome, involved designers from Philips Design and is a good example of collaboration between market researchers and designers to gather feedback on innovative products. The Unihome project involved 300 households and focused on users' experience of using the technologies.

The participants' experiences of the products they used gave the product manufacturers focused, personalised information that could be fed into the refinement and development of those products. At the same time, more general information about the acceptability of this kind of domestic environment was gathered to inform longer-term strategic planning. The next phase of the connected home project involves 2500 households and draws on the lessons learned from the pilot schemes.

1.5.3 Market diffusion

Alongside the development of the product, market research is required to determine the shape of sales strategies and promotional campaigns. The entry of a product into the market, and its spread throughout the market as more and more people buy it, is known as *diffusion*.

Once a product has reached *maturity*, sales strategies may change. Strategies need to be reviewed throughout the life of the product, until the market has bought as much of the product as it is likely to or it is no longer economical to make the product any more.

The diffusion of a product into the market is like dipping a sponge into water. At first the sponge soaks up a little water, then a little more, until finally it reaches saturation point and cannot take any more. This final point is known as *market saturation*. Further market research and customer feedback may initiate changes to the product (adaptation) or may trigger new product development that leads to a replacement product (displacement). The development of radically new replacement products may also be prompted by advances in technology or the availability of new materials. Figure 6 shows the different stages of diffusion as the product reaches more and more of the market.

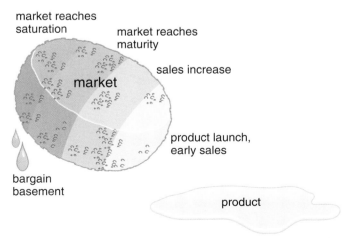

Figure 6 Like a sponge soaking up water, a successful product diffuses into a market until that market reaches saturation

The original Apple iMac (Figure 7a), developed in 1998, was a radical new concept in some ways and an incremental innovation in others. The new concept housed all of the workings of a computer, a DVD drive and a monitor in one, colourful unit. The innards of the iMac were incremental developments of existing technological solutions, although some design challenges were presented by putting all of this into one box.

The product launch of the original iMac used a large television and press advertising campaign. As sales increased later models, which were *incremental developments*, were advertised only in the press. As the

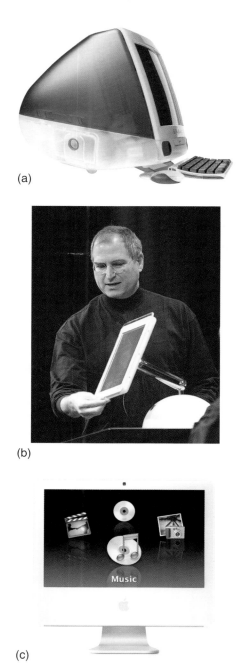

(a)

(b)

(c)

Figure 7 Development of the Apple iMac: (a) original iMac; (b) iMac flat panel being launched in 2002; (c) iMac G5 with the computer and DVD drive built into the screen Sources: Getty Images; Apple Computer Inc

original iMac reached maturity, but before market saturation was reached, the press speculated on a possible replacement, probably fuelled by press releases from Apple.

In 2002 a new flat panel iMac (Figure 7b) was launched with another huge television and press advertising campaign. With this replacement product in place, promotion of the original iMac was left to distributors who used their websites and the specialist computer press. The new iMac eventually displaced the original iMac, although for some time the Original iMac was sold as Apple's cheapest computer. Subsequently the flat panel iMac was replaced by the iMac G5 in 2004 (Figure 7c), and further product development is expected.

1.5.4 Markets and the life of a product

The influence of markets is seen throughout the life of a product, from strategic planning at the early concept stage, when markets and users are the driving force of the new product idea, through to new product development, where market information influences detailed design decisions.

Once a product is ready for launch, promotional campaigns and sales and marketing strategies will be crucial to its successful uptake, and continuing sales and feedback from customers will inform changes and new developments until the product is superseded by a new product altogether. The influence of markets at different stages of the product life cycle is shown on the spiral of innovation in Figure 8.

SAQ 1

What are the three elements common to different definitions of the term market?

SAQ 2

In what ways has the relationship between manufacturer and purchaser or user changed in the past 100 years?

SAQ 3

Three levels at which companies need to consider markets are discussed in 'Importance of markets'. How do these map onto the innovation spiral?

SAQ 4

Explain the terms market diffusion and market saturation.

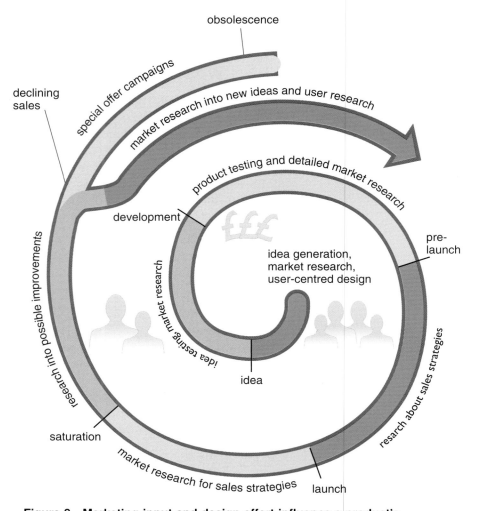

Figure 8   Marketing input and design effort influence a product's development and its subsequent diffusion into the market Source: Open University, 1996

Key points of Section 1

- Markets are an important influence on the development of products and are vital to the success of any new product or innovation.

- The relationships between manufacturers, purchasers and end-users of products have changed over time, and consideration of end-users has now become an important part of the design process.

- There are two aspects to marketing: researching potential markets, and devising sales and marketing strategies to sell products.

- Markets need to be considered at the levels of strategic planning, new product development, and sales strategies and materials.

- The diffusion of new products goes through various stages, until market saturation is reached.

- Markets affect products at all stages of the product life cycle.

2 Who buys products?

2.1 What makes a customer?

The market and the purchasers or customers who might buy products have been discussed, but who are these people? For a company or a person to be considered as a potential market for a product, three criteria need to be satisfied.

1   Do they want it? Do they have an interest in buying the product?

2   Can they afford it? Do they have enough money to buy the product?

3   Do they have access to it? Do they have access to the channels of distribution?

All three of these criteria have to be fulfilled for individuals and groups to be identified as possible markets. People in the developing world may, for example, be interested in a new product but may not have either the money or the access to it to be able to buy it. Others in the developed world may have the money and easy access but will have no interest in the product for practical, aesthetic or social reasons. For example a young person may consider the style too old-fashioned, an environmentalist may have no interest in high energy-use appliances, and a person without a computer is unlikely to be interested in computer software.

By applying the criteria above, the possible market size for a given product can be established – that is, working out what proportion of the population might be interested in the product and have the money and access to it to be able to buy it. It is simply not possible to interview everyone in a country, or even a town, to find out the proportion meeting the criteria. However some of the information needed is quite straightforward to find, at least in general terms.

Information about incomes, savings and credit limits in a country can usually be found in various ways, for example government statistics and information from banking institutions. Information about access to services and geographical distribution can also be found in published statistics, and the company can devise a sales strategy that enables as many people as possible to access the product.

The hardest thing to establish is how many of those people identified as having both money and access might be interested in the proposed product.

To assist with working this out, many companies turn to market sector reports as a source of information. A number of companies specialise in researching, collecting and selling information about different markets to manufacturers and service providers.

Market research reports, such as those produced by Mintel, can be found in specialist libraries or accessed online for a fee. These reports are general in nature – for example in 2004 Mintel produced a report on home delivery shopping. From such general information, an individual company has to work out what its own share of this potential market might be.

All sorts of factors will influence this prediction of market share. Some factors are whether there are competing products, the nature and price of the product and the strength of the company's reputation or brand. More detailed research of the market may be used to help to make these predictions, along with a close examination of competing companies' products and prices.

It is one thing to know the potential size of the market, and another to attract those potential customers to buy the product. As people's expectation of products has become more sophisticated, companies seek to add value to products. In order to add value, market researchers and designers have to understand what people value and desire. Customers often make choices between competing products based on value-added features and the look and feel of a product, particularly if other factors, such as price and performance, are similar. You will learn more about this later in this block.

2.2   Market sectors

So far from this discussion, you may be picturing customers as individual consumers. However the consumer market only accounts for a proportion of all the products sold. Sales from business to business or other organisations account for a significant amount of the overall total.

As Figure 9 shows, the market for products can be divided into four sectors:

- consumer – domestic purchasers

- industrial – companies engaged in manufacturing, processing and engineering

- public – publicly owned organisations, such as government departments, local councils, schools and hospitals

- commercial – service industry purchasers, such as banks, pubs and shops.

Within these sectors there are many different groups or market *segments*, and you will see in Section 3 that different companies aim their products at different segments of the market in order to cope with the competitive environment.

Some products are designed for only one sector – for example an industrial plant and machinery will obviously be sold to specific industries in the industrial sector. Other products are designed to be sold to more than one sector, although the range of products may be tailored to meet the differing requirements of each of these market sectors. A few product types have found markets in all of the above sectors – a good example is microcomputers.

Within any industry there are different markets, each with its own requirements and expectations of a new product. For example a microwave cooker that has been made for the pub and hotel trade may look similar to one made for domestic purchasers (Figure 10) but the commercial customer will be expecting to buy something that is robust, can cope with continual use and is easy to clean, and they will be

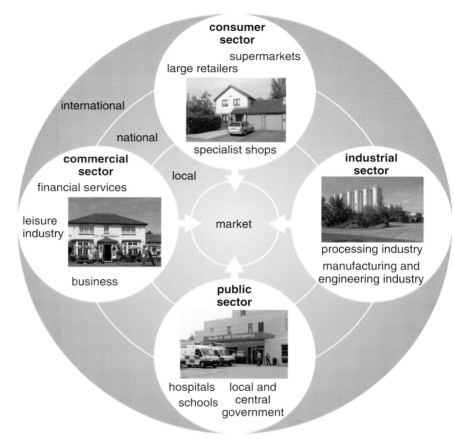

Figure 9 Examples of the four market sectors: consumer, industrial, public, commercial Source: Open University, 1996

prepared to pay for these features. The domestic customer will have similar concerns but they will not be expecting their appliances to take as much wear and tear and so they will expect to pay less. Although the cookers in Figure 10 look similar, Table 1 shows the differences in the specifications for commercial and domestic use.

Table 1 Comparison of features in commercial and domestic microwave cookers

Commercial	Domestic
900–2100 watts	600–900 watts
two magnetrons to produce microwave energy	single magnetron to produce microwave energy
outer casing stainless steel	outer casing painted mild steel
heat mixing system in oven cavity	rotating turntable to distribute heat
oven size based on standard-size dishes used in catering	oven size based on domestic food preparation
built for heavy use	built for use a couple of times a day

The resin cast in Figure 11 is an example of a medical technology for the public sector. The innovative new materials for this cast were made by 3M Industries. The material is a bandage impregnated with resin. When the bandage is soaked in lukewarm water, the resin is activated. The patient can be bandaged and the resin will set within 20 minutes.

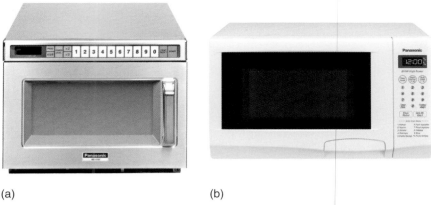

(a)   (b)

Figure 10   (a) Microwave cooker designed for commercial use. (b) Domestic microwave cooker from the same manufacturer Source: Panansonic UK Ltd.

Figure 11   Scotchcast Plus resin cast Source: 3M UK

Once set the cast is light, hard and will repel water, offering a strong advantage over conventional plaster casts that can take many hours to set and are vulnerable to water penetration.

In addition to being clear about which market sectors they are aiming at, all companies have to make decisions about where they will sell their products geographically – for example whether they will concentrate on sales to specific countries or regions, and whether their main business will be based on the home market, on exports or on a combination of both. Such decisions will affect the design of the product because of differences not only of cultures in different countries but also because of differences in legislation and technical requirements.

2.3   Supply and distribution chains

The term supply chain describes the passing of components and products between manufacturers and other agents until they reach the purchaser at the end of the chain. Supply chains are usually complex, involving many components manufacturers to arrive at one finished product. Even a simple non-technical product like a pencil will require the sourcing of wood, graphite, paints and glues from different companies, which, in their turn, sourced the ingredients and materials needed to process them.

For the purposes of this block, I will look only at the supply chain from the finished product to the end-user, which is referred to as the distribution chain. The supply chain will vary between market sectors – for example a complex industrial or public sector product like a piece of production machinery or a train will not reach the purchaser in the same way as a consumer or commercial sector product.

Consumer purchases are usually supplied through a retailer, the internet or mail order. By contrast, commercial, industrial and public sector purchases are most often made through wholesalers or agents acting for the manufacturer, although some large purchases may be made directly from the manufacturer (Figure 12).

Small- to medium-sized manufacturing companies with a small sales team often use wholesalers or agents to sell their products. They also use these agents to find out about customer needs. Wholesalers either sell the product to the final purchaser or, in the case of consumer goods, the product is sold on to a retailer who will sell the goods on to their final destination. However large retailers such as major supermarket chains and stores may make purchases directly from the manufacturer or even commission products for their exclusive sale – these are known as super-retailers.

The longer the chain of distributors, the greater the number of people who have to be convinced of the value of a product. If a wholesaler does not see a product as worth stocking, potential consumers may never have a chance to decide for themselves. So the chain of distribution will affect how new products are launched and how information on the success of existing products is gathered, and will generally inform the marketing campaigns and sales strategies used by the company.

Sometimes distributors are a source of new product ideas. For example wholesalers who distribute goods for a number of competing companies may be able to give feedback to companies on how their products compare and why some are more successful than others. In industries that do not carry out extensive market research, this feedback from wholesalers is invaluable.

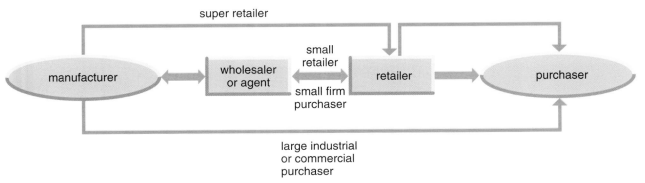

Figure 12 Distribution chains from manufacturer to purchaser

2.4   Purchasers and users

You will have seen above that there are a number of different parties involved before the final purchase of a product is made. However it is important to realise that the *purchaser* of a product and the *end user* may not necessarily be the same person. Indeed the majority of purchases in the commercial, industrial and public sectors will be made by someone in the organisation, for use by employees who may not have been involved in the purchasing decision.

Even in the consumer sector, purchases are often made by someone other than the end user – for example when gifts are given or purchases are made on behalf of children or relatives. The distinction between purchaser and end user can be important when carrying out market research and planning sales strategies. If the purchaser is different from the end user, this could have implications for product design as well as for sales strategies.

Many purchasing decisions, such as buying expensive items like large pieces of furniture, white goods and cars, will be made jointly by the adults in a household. The implication of this is that manufacturers need to be aware of the features looked for by both male and female customers.

For example, in the past, the sales literature and methods for selling vacuum cleaners were designed to emphasise the technical specification, for the benefit of male customers, who were considered to be more interested in such details. Whereas the ease of use, efficiency and performance of the machine were emphasised for the benefit of women, who were thought to be more likely to be interested in those aspects.

Current demographic changes, such as an increasing number of single-parent and single-person households, may affect the design and sales of such products in the future. Manufacturers watch such trends closely and will periodically review their product development and marketing strategies.

2.5   Relationships between manufacturers and purchasers

The strength and nature of the relationships between manufacturing companies and purchasers are determined to some extent by the nature of the industry, the product and the distribution chain. Some of the forms this relationship might take are as follows.

2.5.1 Indirect relationships

In the consumer products sector throughout most of the twentieth century, there was little direct relationship between the purchaser and the manufacturer. This was due to the many links in the chain between purchaser and manufacturer. Manufacturing companies relied on intermediaries such as wholesalers or specialist market research companies to gather information about the market.

However, to some extent, this has changed in recent years. This is partly due to the rise of super-retailers and their use of electronic data collection, which has enabled more sophisticated gathering and analysis of data. It is also increasingly common to find manufacturing companies adopting a user-centred approach and involving consumers in the product development process directly, as you will see in Section 5.

2.5.2 Commissioning relationships

In the commercial, industrial and public sectors large purchasers often commission or procure particular products from manufacturers. Whether commissioning is appropriate depends on the size of the order placed and the nature of the product. In the industrial sector, a company may commission a specialist large machine tool, or even an entire production plant, directly because such items are one-off, high-value purchases. However the light fittings for the same company may more appropriately be bought 'off the peg' through a wholesaler.

The commissioning of a product entails the purchaser going to a manufacturer with a specific set of needs and requirements (product specification) the manufacturer is asked to meet. A commissioned product may simply be a customised version of a product already made and sold by that manufacturer, or it might be a new product the manufacturer has the expertise and facilities to develop.

Manufacturers frequently commission parts and components from specialist manufacturers to be assembled into their own products. For example a manufacturing company may commission a microchip from a specialist chip manufacturer, a purpose-made rubber seal from another manufacturer and specialist fixings from another company.

For some complex products a group of manufacturers may be involved, each commissioned to work on various aspects of the product and to coordinate their efforts to create a satisfactory whole. For example in the transport industry the design and build of new locomotives and rolling stock for a train operating company will involve a train manufacturer working with a large number of components manufacturers to supply parts, many of which may have to be custom built.

Companies that have commissioned products work closely with the manufacturer to ensure the final product matches the original specifications. Commissioning relationships can exist in all market sectors. In the consumer sector some purchasers may commission pieces directly from manufacturers, particularly furnishings and bespoke items for the house. However, one step further up the supply chain, many retailers commission their own brand versions of all sorts of goods, such as baked beans, ready meals and household goods. An example of a retailer who offers own-brand products is the supermarket chain Lidl. The company commissions a range of goods for sale in its shops across Europe, from own-brand food through to tea towel holders and computers.

In recent years a new form of the commissioning relationship has evolved. Known as *mass customisation*, the potential purchaser customises their purchases using a range of options offered by the manufacturer. Mass customisation has been adopted by many car companies and uses the opportunities offered by the internet for customer and manufacturer to communicate directly through the company website, where customers can place their order. The potential purchaser of a car is able to choose from different engine sizes, transmissions, colours, upholstery materials, seats, accessories and features. This enables the purchaser to 'build' the car they would like from the options available.

However mass customisation is about more than offering consumers choice. From the manufacturers' point of view, building a car to exact requirements when a sale has been made enables a more efficient production process and avoids the build-up of large quantities of stock. Within the factory, mass customisation presents the challenge of creating an automated system that ensures that individual products are built to the specification of the user. These production systems are developing and evolving, and it is likely that in the future an increasing number of products will be ordered and built in this way.

2.5.3 Joint development

Manufacturers producing goods for the commercial, industrial or public sector may consult selected customers about their requirements and wishes when they are planning new products. This consultation may be carried out in various ways. In many companies it will be an informal process, whereby someone in the company is charged with talking to key customers. In other companies the process may be more formal, for example setting up a panel to discuss a new product idea. Box 1 shows an example from the public sector where consultations with customers led to the development of an innovative product.

Box 1   Haldo bollards

A British company called Haldo makes illuminated traffic bollards, which can be found on roads in the UK. This company works closely with local government officers to develop and improve its products.

(a)

(b)

Figure 13   Road bollards: (a) recent model made from springy plastic; (b) old model made with metal springs Source: Haldo

The bollard in Figure 13(a) was created in consultation with customers. The main features of this bollard are its slim shape and its bendability.

The bollard exploits the springiness of the plastic from which it is made, to spring back if hit.

Haldo's first bollard in the 1960s (Figure 13b) had similar characteristics but the springiness was achieved through metal springs that would eventually wear. This type of bollard was discontinued in the 1970s in favour of the ubiquitous square bollard, which was more robust. However consultations with customers in the 1990s showed a need for bollards that could be used in situations where maximum visibility was important, such as on traffic islands, where a square bollard might obscure a child. Haldo revisited its earlier concept, applying the knowledge of plastics that had been developed in the interim.

Joint development is sometimes found in the design of consumer products but may not always involve the consumer directly. Two companies may work together on developing different aspects of a product or collaborate on innovations in production technology. For example Philips, as a global electronics manufacturer, has worked with clothing companies Levi and Nike to create wearable electronics (Figure 14). With Levi the collaborations produced jackets that contain phones, music players and headphones. With Nike the collaboration produced a range of clip-on music players and integral body monitors for use when exercising. In these cases Philips carried out extensive user research to determine what users wished for and the characteristics those products should have.

Figure 14   Wearable electronics Source: Philips Electronics UK Ltd

2.6   Market segmentation

Markets sectors are broad categories. However for the development of individual products more detailed information is needed. So to assist the design and development process, marketing professionals think of each market sector as being divided into smaller segments, in which the purchasers have similar characteristics and tastes.

The idea of market segmentation within a sector was created in the 1920s by Alfred P. Sloan to help General Motors to compete with Ford's Model T car. The Model T came in only one colour and model so General Motors chose to develop a range of possible models 'for every purse and person'. The result was the basic Chevrolet available in a number of colours, two kinds of Buick aimed at the family motorist, and the luxury Cadillac. The strategy was so successful that the Model T could not compete and General Motors took over from Ford as the major US car manufacturer.

Segmentation has become more and more sophisticated as more is understood about people and their lifestyles. However similar market segments are still being used by the car industry today, as you can see in Figure 15.

(a)

(b)

(c)

Figure 15   Range of cars from the same manufacturer aimed at different market segments Source: Ford Motor Company Limited

Exercise 3   Segments within the consumer sector

Can you think of some of the ways markets might be segmented in the consumer sector?

Discussion

Companies view their market segments in different ways depending on the nature of their business. However some of the common classifications that are made include the following:

- income – low, medium, high

- profession – professional, skilled, manual

- age group – young, middle-aged, elderly

- family – single, couple with no children, couple with one child/several children, couple with grown up-children, single parent

- geography – city dwellers, country dwellers, suburbanites, from various regions in the UK, continental Europeans, markets on other continents.

Essentially, market segmentation is a way of categorising potential purchasers into groups. The starting point for classification may be a measurable factor, such as age or income, or one of the other factors mentioned in Exercise 3. Frequently, however, a combination of these measurable factors may be used to identify potential markets, for example age plus geographical location – such as people aged between 18 and 25, living in a city.

Within the groups identified by measurable factors, further groupings based on lifestyle and interests can be identified. Designers, like marketers, develop their own terms to describe different users. For example at Philips Design, a 'plugged-in' person is shorthand for a young person who enjoys and frequently uses electronic gadgets and the internet. Other examples of lifestyle groups are 'empty nesters' (middle-aged people with money whose children have grown up and left home), 'active elderly' and 'city chic'. These market groups are identified and drawn up into *profiles* by the marketing department. These profiles are used to brief the design team.

For the consumer market, the following factors are frequently used to segment the market:

- geographical location – where potential purchasers live, such as country or city

- psychographic factors – how people see themselves and the world around them, such as status conscious or environmentalist

- behavioural factors – what people do, such as angler, painter or ballroom dancer

- demographic factors – such as age or income (Figure 16).

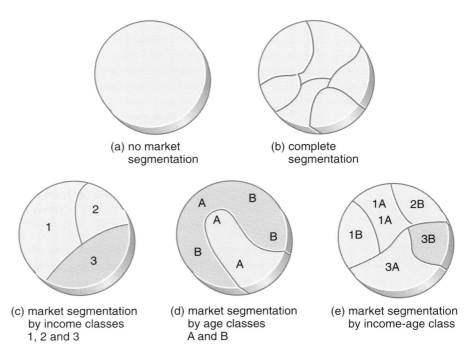

(a) no market segmentation

(b) complete segmentation

(c) market segmentation by income classes 1, 2 and 3

(d) market segmentation by age classes A and B

(e) market segmentation by income-age class

Figure 16 Different segmentations of a market Source: adapted from Kotler, 1988

For commercial, industrial and public sector markets, segmentation takes *geographical location* into account but different factors are used to identify market segments such as:

- type of organisation – segmenting the market according to the main business of the organisation

- company size

- product use – segmenting the market according to how the product would be used

- usage rate – segmenting the market according to the quantities of the product that would be ordered, for example one-off or regular orders.

SAQ 5

What are the four main market sectors? Give an example of each sector.

SAQ 6

What are the links in the distribution chain for consumer goods? How does this differ from the distribution chain for commercial products?

SAQ 7

What is the role of the wholesaler/agent in the chain of distribution? How might this affect the design of new products?

SAQ 8

Identify three possible forms of relationship between manufacturers and purchasers in the product development process.

2.7 How many and how much?

As well as knowing who is likely to buy their product, manufacturers also have to know the quantity they are likely to sell. Different products require different sizes of market, determined by the nature of the product, its price and the production processes used.

2.7.1 High cost, low volume

In some industries there is one-off commissioning of high-cost artefacts. In such situations, the cost of creating the necessary tools to make the product will be part of the costing of the product as a whole. In other industries, such as luxury cars, production might take place in small batches.

2.7.2 Low cost, high volume

In other industries, the cost of creating new tools will have to be justified by the expected volume of sales. For example the cost of creating a new mould for injection moulding a plastic component can be tens of thousands of pounds. When this is the case companies have to consider how many of the product are likely to be sold and at what price, and whether sufficient profit will be made.

As a rule the lower the price of a product, the greater the volume of sales must be. Products produced on continuous or near-continuous production lines, such as light bulbs, foodstuffs and chemicals, are usually low-cost, high-volume products.

2.7.3 Medium cost, medium volume

In some industries, products may be produced in large quantities on assembly lines – this is most often the case for consumer white goods such as washing machines and fridges. These are usually products of medium cost and medium sales volume.

2.7.4 Variable cost, variable volume

Although the broad categories of production process seen above are still common, the introduction of computer-controlled production has allowed a more flexible approach to production. With computer-controlled processes, variations in products may be made at relatively low cost, allowing greater choice and flexibility. You have already encountered the concept of mass customisation in the car industry as an up-and-coming approach in manufacture.

Although not all companies use computer-controlled processes to create customised products, many use these processes to respond to the demands of the marketplace, for example adjusting the numbers of products made in a particular colour in response to how well that colour is selling.

2.7.5 Importance to designers

These production issues are important factors that a designer must take into account when designing and developing a new product. It is important to know what the end cost of the product should be, what the anticipated volume of sales is and how the product will be produced. In large companies the briefing of designers for a new product will almost always include representatives from both marketing and production, reflecting the need for these factors to be taken into account from the beginning of the development process.

Exercise 4   Effect of production type on design

Think of examples of each of the approaches to production listed above. In what ways do you think designs might be affected by the approach chosen?

Discussion

Table 2 has some further examples.

Table 2   Production approaches and suitable products

Production approach	Suitable product
high cost, low volume	production plant, bespoke cars, haute couture fashion, medical equipment such as MRI scanners, locomotives, specialist machine tools
low cost, high volume	toothbrushes, batteries, paperclips, safety pins, CDs
medium cost, medium volume	computers, DVD players, microwave ovens, cameras
variable cost, variable volume	furniture, some toys, fashion accessories

The nature of the production process will affect the choice of materials and components, which will in turn affect the design. For example items intended to be injection moulded need to be designed for this process. With this process the join lines and the nipples, where the mould separates from the tool, need to be carefully located for both aesthetic and functional reasons (Figure 17).

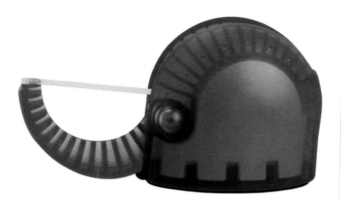

Figure 17 Injection moulded, translucent tape dispenser with internal ribs visible. The ribs give mechanical strength and add to the aesthetic appeal.
Source: Julian Brown

Other factors that need to be considered are how well the design can be reproduced in quantity, whether the characteristics of the materials or components are consistent, and does the production process require particular skills of those making it, to achieve the intended outcome? For example a bespoke car may be made or finished by hand to achieve its engineering and aesthetic qualities, whereas a DVD player requires precision engineering of the production plant to enable it to be reproduced in quantity.

For electronic products and other finely engineered products for the mass market, the design of the production plant is a critical part of the implementation of innovation. This is the concern of the production engineers rather than the product designer, although the designer will often work with production colleagues to ensure the desired outcomes are achieved.

Key points of Section 2

- For a market to exist the potential purchasers must have sufficient money, interest in the product and access to the channels of distribution.

- There are four main market sectors: consumer, commercial, industrial and public.

- Different chains of distribution are appropriate to different products and industries.

- In all sectors it cannot be assumed the purchaser and the end-user are the same person.

- There are three kinds of relationship between manufacturers and purchasers: indirect, commissioning and joint development.

- Within each market sector, companies identify groups or market segments to target their research and sales effort. Common factors for identifying market segments in the consumer sector are geography, psychographics, behaviour and demographics. For commercial, industrial and public sectors the factors are geographical location, type of organisation, company size, product use and usage rate.

- The costs and volumes of production vary according to the nature of products. Generally the fewer items produced, the higher the cost. However modern production techniques now allow some products to be made at variable cost and volume.

3 Ways of finding out about markets

3.1 Role of marketing

Companies find out about their potential customers in a number of different ways. Research into potential markets and customers used to be the exclusive domain of a marketing department. However over the past few decades, the role of marketing departments within companies has evolved and changed. Departments used to work independently on their own area of interest, for example finance, production and marketing. Now, however, many companies take a more integrated approach to product development, and the marketing department takes the role of mediator between the customer and the other departments of the company (Figure 18).

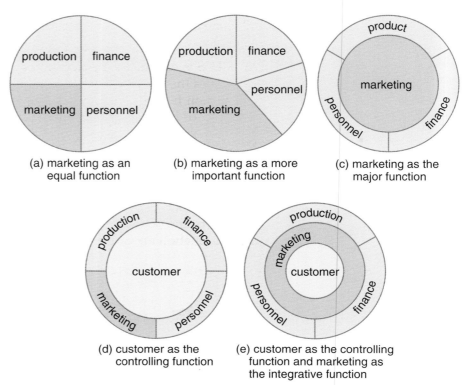

Figure 18   **Evolution of the position of marketing in the development process. In this simplified model, design is considered as part of the production function.** Source: adapted from Kotler (1988)

The terms marketing and sales are often used interchangeably, because marketing is seen as being all about selling a product. This is of course the primary concern of the marketing department. However, as products have evolved and purchasers have become more sophisticated, marketing departments have become involved at all stages of the development process.

Marketers now have an input from the initial briefing through to the detailed design stage and beyond. This involvement is also about selling products, through bringing an awareness of market requirements into the design process to make more attractive products and develop a strong brand.

Crucial to the early stages of any product development is the initial market research, which addresses such crucial questions as:

- Who are the potential purchasers?

- What problems are perceived with existing products?

- What sorts of products do potential purchasers want?

3.2 Marketing decision support systems

To make informed decisions about existing products and possible areas for innovation, companies need to gather information on their potential customers and their needs and to set this information in the context of cultures and trends in society. As the amount of information available on markets has become more complex and sophisticated, large companies have set up a marketing decision support system (MDSS) to integrate and disseminate information to decision-makers within the company.

An MDSS is essentially a collection of data, systems, tools and techniques that an organisation uses to gather and interpret information from the company and its environment (Figure 19). This collection of information and tools is used to inform market decisions and strategies.

In a large company the MDSS is likely to be on a computer system run by the marketing department. However in smaller companies, where the collection of data is carried out by a small team or an individual, the information might simply be kept on one or two personal computers and in a filing cabinet. In even smaller companies much of this information about markets may be kept inside someone's head.

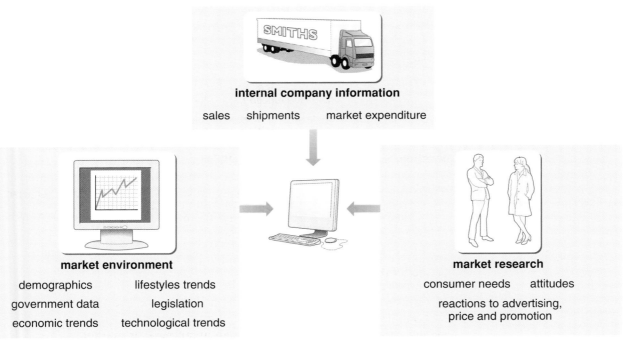

internal company information

sales   shipments   market expenditure

market environment

demographics   lifestyles trends

government data   legislation

economic trends   technological trends

market research

consumer needs   attitudes

reactions to advertising,
price and promotion

Figure 19   Sources of information for the marketing decision support system Source: Open University, 1996

The information collected by the company informs all three company activities identified in Section 1.

- *Strategic plan.* Market information about trends in society and advances in technology is used to inform decisions taken at board level about company strategies for future product development.

- *New product development.* Information collected about consumer needs and desires should reach all those involved in the development of new products and innovations.

- *Sales and marketing strategy.* Information collected about how existing products are perceived and how effective sales strategies were should reach all those involved in marketing and sales to help them to shape their promotional strategy.

The MDSS contains information from three sources:

- *Internal company information.* There will be data on retail sales, shipments, the supply chain and the cost of marketing campaigns. This information is gathered from relevant departments to provide marketing managers with data about income and costs so that the profitability of products can be analysed. Most of this data is quantitative in the form of figures and statistics.

- *Information about the market environment.* This includes information about demographic changes, lifestyle trends, family roles, government and regulations, economic factors, technological trends and competitors' products.

  Information on the market environment is relatively unstructured in comparison to the internal company and market research information. Rather than relying on databases or formal studies, this is a loose network of information, which is channelled to a manager or department to review for insights or trends. A wide range of secondary sources of information, such as government reports, journal articles, websites and trade magazines, are used. Large companies usually keep a library of this sort of information.

  There are companies that specialise in scanning for this information on the market environment and that sell their services to subscribing companies. This information comprises a combination of quantitative and qualitative data.

- *Information from primary market research.* Information will be collected about consumer needs, attitudes towards the company's products, reactions to advertising, price and promotional strategies.

  Consumer studies are often used to get information from primary sources. Studies of this kind may be carried out by the marketing department within the manufacturing company itself, but many companies pay for the services of a market research firm or advertising agency to gather this information on their behalf. This information often comprises a combination of quantitative and qualitative data.

3.2.1 Main tasks of a marketing decision support system

The main tasks of an MDSS can be categorised as follows:

- Market analysis

  Forecasting and monitoring sales, identifying target markets, defining the characteristics of the market, looking for new ideas.

- Product research

  Assessing product acceptance, determining customer preferences, carrying out packaging trials.

- Distribution research

  Identifying the best sales outlets and monitoring sales through the distribution channels used.

- Price research

  Looking at competitors' prices, determining what price the market will bear and assessing the price that will generate the optimum volume of sales and profit.

- Promotion research

  Identifying the most effective ways of communicating with potential customers, testing customer reactions to advertising ideas and existing advertisements.

- Market testing

  Assessing trial marketing of new products looking at customer behaviour and sales performance.

Exercise 5   What are the information needs?

Think about the needs of companies operating in different market sectors. Do you think the information gathered in the MDSS will be different?

Discussion

The internal company information is likely to be similar irrespective of the sector in which a company is operating. This is because much of this information is quantitative and shows how well a company is performing.

Information from the market environment may vary, although demographic data could be important in the commercial sector and possibly in the public sector too – for example a company planning a new form of public transport would be interested in who the likely users might be. Government data, regulations, economic factors and technological trends are important in every sector, as is knowledge of competing or similar products.

Information from primary market research can be important in all market sectors. Manufacturing companies operating in the commercial, industrial and public sectors often have close relationships with the organisations, companies and institutions in their target market sectors. This enables the manufacturing company to find out directly what its requirements are.

Sometimes within those target sectors, it may be important to look at the needs of the people who will be using the product (end users), while at the same time establishing the requirements of the purchasing departments who make the decision to buy. For example the development of a piece of medical equipment may require a company to find out what patients and practitioners need, while meeting the price criteria set by the health authorities.

Researching attitudes towards the company's products and reactions to advertising, pricing and promotional strategies may be done in different ways in different sectors but this information is always important to help companies to understand why products succeed or fail.

3.3 Understanding the market environment

For any product to succeed it is essential for the company to understand and analyse the wider environment within which the company is developing its products. This is true wherever those products are on the spectrum of innovation, whether they are radical innovations or incrementally improved products. In Section 2 you met the concept of market segmentation. The information used to create these conceptual segmentations of the market is largely drawn from the sources of information discussed below.

Some of the areas of information I describe below are of greater relevance to the development of consumer products, but areas such as environmental legislation, economic factors and technological trends are equally important across all sectors. Even lifestyle and demographic changes affect all sectors to a greater or lesser extent, for example through the changing characteristics of the workforce such as age and skills.

3.3.1 Information about societal trends

The three areas of information described immediately below are about consumers: who they are, how they think and how they live. The information gathered may be used to get a picture of different market segments and to create tools such as profiles or personas that can be used by designers in the design and development process to help them to focus on the needs and desires of identified groups. You will learn more about this in Section 4.

Demographics

This is the study of population and is important for both successful innovation and new product development. Demographics looks at changes in the population as a whole, for example age, gender balance, ethnic origins, disability and illness. It is concerned with where people live, the balance between urban and rural populations, and the wealth groups of people have available to them.

The implications of demographic changes need to be considered carefully by companies when designing products. In the UK, for example, an awareness of an ageing population is beginning to show itself in the range of products available. Analysing demographic changes can be a good stimulus to new product development.

A range of user-friendly power tools was designed by Matthew Wright, a research associate at the Helen Hamlyn Research Centre for Inclusive Design at the Royal College of Art. Figure 20 shows an example of a sanding tool. The stimulus for this development was a

Figure 20 Hand sander developed for the elderly Source: Helen Hamlyn Research Centre

report from the Henley Centre for Social Forecasting, which showed that spending on power tools rose when people reached retirement age but then declined among older people because of difficulties in using the tools. The brief was to design tools suitable for older users that would benefit all users. You can see the full Design Council case study on the T211 DVD.

Lifestyle changes

Lifestyle changes are about psychological matters such as people's attitudes to themselves and the world around them, and are sometimes referred to as *psychographic* changes. For example the adoption of sportswear as fashion, coupled with the trend of taking exercise in gyms and leisure centres, has led to the development of electronic accessories. An example is the Philips-Nike PSA mini MP3 player that you saw in Section 1.

Other lifestyle trends, such as increased environmental awareness, especially in some western European countries, have affected not just consumer products but also commercial and industrial ones. One example is the increased use of environmentally friendly, energy-saving lighting and heating systems. Human beings are complex creatures, and adoption of such systems may be a result of more than one motive, such as a desire to cut costs or comply with government legislation as well as a concern for the environment.

Family roles

Family roles are related to both lifestyle and demographic changes. The roles adopted within families influence the development of products, and an understanding of who does what in the home is important for the planning of consumer products and marketing strategies. For example it may be important to know whether household tasks are seen as the responsibility of particular family members.

Family roles are undoubtedly affected by demographic changes – for example an increase in the number of single-parent and divorced families in the UK means there are more households in which the lone occupant has to do all of the household chores themselves.

Social sciences

The discipline of marketing has drawn on the knowledge of psychologists for many years. However, in the 1990s, some leading design companies involved in the product development process began to look towards other social science disciplines for a more in-depth understanding of the people for whom they were designing. In some companies the knowledge of anthropologists, ethnographers and psychologists is now added to the body of information in the marketing decision support system. The expertise of these disciplines is used particularly to assist designers in understanding how individuals and groups relate to objects, how they use and adapt to products and what they perceive as important and valuable.

3.3.2 Trends, legislation and scientific advances

In addition to this information about people there are a number of other kinds of information that are monitored and collected by companies.

Economic trends

Economic trends are keenly watched by all manufacturers at both a macro- and a micro-level. The UK government produces many publications that chart the fortunes of various industries over the course of each year in terms of imports and exports. The government's Department of Trade and Industry publishes statistics that give information on broad economic trends. An understanding of economic trends will help a company to plan investments and products that are appropriate to the economic climate.

Government legislation, regulations and standards

Companies need to be aware of the legislation and regulations in any countries in which they wish to operate. They also need to be aware of the likely timing of legislative changes, so that they can plan for changes well in advance. An example of government legislation and its effect on product design is legislation that demanded a decrease in car exhaust emissions. In the UK, legislation of this kind was introduced in stages, to enable car manufacturers, who plan new cars several years ahead, to anticipate the changes required and allow for them in the development process. Failure to keep track of government legislation could cause a company to lose time and forfeit its competitive edge.

Companies also have to be aware of the legislation that varies from country to country and, in the case of the United States of America, from state to state. A simple example of this is that each country has its own requirements for the configuration of car headlights, so that adjustments have to be made when cars are imported. Products have to be designed to meet the requirements of any country in which the company wishes to operate or sell.

Technological trends and scientific advances

Trends in technology and materials are monitored to keep abreast of possibilities both for new products and for new production processes. The 1990s, for example, saw the use of laser technology in an increasingly wide range of products and production processes, and developments in materials have led to products that would not previously have been possible. An example of this is the development of DVDs, which in the early twenty-first century went from being high-cost, exclusive items to being ubiquitous, low-cost products within a short space of time.

Companies have to try to distinguish the most important technological trends from the wealth of developments that present themselves. Getting it wrong could mean investment in a product that is not compatible with anyone else's product.

Companies routinely monitor the competition to plan new product development and marketing strategies. Some companies like to lead the field in new product development, while others are content to let those leading companies break the ground. Most manufacturing companies routinely examine their competitors' catalogues, published company accounts and patents, and even take apart (reverse engineer) their products.

Companies can be very inventive in finding ways around patents to produce their own version of a successful product. An example of this can be seen in the vacuum cleaner market, where the bagless Dyson cyclonic range of cleaners rapidly gained market dominance. Competing manufacturers were stimulated to respond with their own designs for bagless vacuum cleaners.

Case study   NanoCool ice pack

Cool Logistics is an established company that has been making ice packs for use in the pharmaceutical industry since the 1980s. In 2001 it came across information about a scientific discovery that could radically alter its products.

The discovery, by an American called Douglas Smith, was a material that absorbed water without changing in volume.

The discovery enabled Cool Logistics to create the NanoCool unit. This unit is incorporated into the lid of an insulated container, taking up much less space than conventional ice packs (Figure 21). The technology is based on a vacuum absorption process that is triggered by a push-button actuator. Modified water is released in the direction of the food-safe material discovered by Smith. The water is absorbed, causing a drop in temperature inside the package to between 2°C and 8°C.

Although the temperature of the absorbing material rises, heat is ducted away from the goods being transported. The warmer the temperature outside the packaging, the harder the product works. The method is claimed to be seven times more efficient than using ice.

Cool Logistics invited its customers to come and try out the new technology, which was housed in a silver paper container featuring a solitary button. When the curious guests of Cool Logistics pressed this button, they triggered a process that within a short time led to ice forming on the outside of one side of the prototype.

The guests were impressed and wanted to place orders. After 2 years of development and testing, the product was launched onto the market in 2003.

Figure 21   NanoCool ice pack Source: Direction Consultants

One of the main advantages for would-be customers is substantial cost savings. Up to 15 per cent of transport costs could be saved because the NanoCool packs take up only a quarter of the space of conventional ice packs. The NanoCool packs can also be stored on a shelf for up to a year, eliminating the need to maintain expensive chilling facilities.

Initially Cool Logistics will focus on the low-volume, high-value market offered by pharmaceuticals transport, but the future could see manufacturing scaled-up to handle altogether larger commodity markets.

The comments of Cool Logistics director Bill Hollin show how important customer requirements were to this product development:

> The main reason for products not succeeding is failure to understand customer requirements. If you know the market and you have your customers' assistance, you know what they want because they've told you. You have to decide whether you're able to give it to them – we focused on that from the start.

> If you have areas where you don't satisfy customer requirements, you put your product development effort into those areas. For instance our customers wanted to know how they could tell the product was working, so we introduced temperature-sensitive paint to indicate when it was.

(Source: adapted from Design Council, undated)

SAQ 9

What is the marketing decision support system and why is it important?

SAQ 10

Companies collect information on a number of different trends. What are these trends? Can you think of any more examples?

3.4 Market research

The marketing decision support system gathers information from a wide range of sources. One of the important sources of information for this system is market research. This is often used as a blanket term to refer to a wide range of activities concerned with the gathering and evaluation of information. However in this section the term will be used to mean the collection of information from *primary sources* – research with potential purchasers.

Market research is used in several different ways:

- to generate new ideas
- to evaluate the market potential or acceptability of products at various stages of development
- to develop ideas into products that fit market requirements
- to help to formulate marketing strategies to promote products.

Market research is a particularly important source of information for the commercial and consumer market sectors, although some form of market research is found in every market sector. Researching the market may be a formal or an informal process – for example informal consultation with customers may take place at trade shows or during site visits, whereas formal market research might entail the distribution and quantitative analysis of responses to a survey.

Companies often commission specialist market research companies to conduct formal market research because this approach demands particular skills and knowledge, as well as access to information such as databases of potential customers. Some market research companies specialise in producing market reports about general trends in society. Many manufacturers use the information in such reports to guide their plans.

In a large company, briefings based on market research reports may provide the starting point for designers seeking to improve existing products or develop new ones. For a small company with limited resources, market research may be limited to discussions with interested parties and an observation of current trends.

Some of the general reasons for researching the market are given in Table 3. As you can see, the aims of research are quite different at different points of product development. Most large companies carry out all of these forms of research at some point, particularly for innovative products.

Market research projects can be exploratory, descriptive, explanatory or predictive.

Exploratory projects adopt a qualitative approach to identifying and understanding market issues – in other words such projects aim to explore, or get a feel for, the market.

Descriptive projects take a more structured and quantitative approach to finding out about such aspects of the market as determining consumer attitudes and price barriers. Essentially, such projects are describing the existing market situation.

Table 3   Reasons for researching the market at different stages of product life

Aim of research	When carried out
identify new markets, segments, groups or individuals	product planning, initial stages before concept design
identify problems with existing products or requirements of new products	product planning or concept design stages
test developed products	at prototype stage or sometimes after the product has started being sold
understand user or purchaser experience post-purchase	after individual purchases; for incremental product development, research may be carried out when a product is reaching maturity
understand perceptions of relationship with company	research of this kind may be carried out at any time because it is concerned with perceptions of the company rather than individual products

Explanatory projects focus on trying to find explanations for why certain events are happening, such as declining market share.

Predictive projects employ quantitative techniques to try to predict the outcome of marketing decisions, for example forecasting the expected level of sales.

Each of these approaches is appropriate at different times and in different situations. The first three approaches may be particularly useful from a design perspective. The kinds of information that may be gained are an understanding of users' preferences, such as likes and dislikes, and explanations about why previous products have succeeded or failed, which may inform the design of product features, performance and safety.

Exercise 6   Which market research approach?

Which of the four market research approaches might be most appropriate when looking at:

- a radically new product
- an existing product
- a product that has been incrementally developed and is going to be relaunched
- a product that is not selling as well as it used to
- several possible marketing strategies?

Spend a few minutes thinking about this before reading the discussion below.

Discussion

The exploratory approach might be adopted when considering radically new products.

The descriptive approach might be appropriate later, to identify the market after a new product has been developed, although it may also be used with an existing product when a decision has been made to relaunch the product. The information gathered will be used to inform the pricing and promotion strategies.

The explanatory approach might be used when existing products are not selling as well as they have in the past or when new products are not selling as well as anticipated.

The predictive approach is used to look at the likely economic success of various strategies for selling the product, and could be used either for new products or for existing ones when new strategies are being considered.

3.5   Quantitative and qualitative information

In the description of the different market research approaches above, I have described techniques as being qualitative or quantitative. The terms themselves give a clue to their meaning. Quantitative information is about quantities, in other words hard facts and statistics. Qualitative information is about qualities, values and opinions.

Research based on quantitative techniques seeks to obtain hard data about purchaser behaviour, for example to estimate the size of the market or gauge the success of marketing campaigns in certain areas by looking at sales figures. Quantitative research questions are usually closed questions with a limited choice of responses. The numerical analysis of the data collected is often computerised, although the interpretation of these statistics is made by the researchers. This kind of research is sometimes referred to as traditional marketing.

Research based on qualitative techniques is used for such purposes as evaluating product proposals, generating ideas for products and finding out about purchasers' attitudes. Qualitative research questions are often open-ended, and the responses have to be interpreted and analysed by the researcher. Qualitative research is also sometimes referred to as creative marketing.

The main difference between qualitative and quantitative research is that qualitative research seeks to develop an in-depth understanding of potential purchasers and users, whereas quantitative research looks at markets as a whole and collects statistically significant data and figures to inform decisions and expectations about such things as the volume of sales.

Exercise 7   Qualitative and quantitative information

Have you been stopped in the street and asked questions, been sent postal or internet surveys or been asked to take part in a telephone survey? Do you think the information gathered in such surveys is qualitative or quantitative?

Alternatively have you ever taken part in a focus group or been interviewed individually for your opinions on a product or service? Is the information gathered in an open-ended interview or group situation generally qualitative or quantitative?

Discussion

Any survey that has a limited range of choices for the responses is a quantitative survey. You may have received postal surveys that have included long lists of questions about such things as your preferred newspaper, the car you drive, and so on. In recent years internet surveys have become quite popular with market research companies and the information gathered can be analysed almost instantaneously, in some cases offering you the option to see how your responses compare with those of all the other respondents who have taken the survey.

Occasionally surveys use open-ended questions to obtain qualitative data as well as quantitative data. However this is rarer when a large number of people are being surveyed because the analysis of qualitative data demands a lot of time and thought.

Increasingly telephone surveys are being used to collect data too, although some calls claiming to be telephone surveys are actually a form of sales contact.

Focus groups and individual interviews that seek to find out more about your own personal experience and opinions are usually gathering qualitative information.

3.6 Carrying out valid research

In order to be of any significance market research has to be conducted rigorously. This applies to both qualitative and quantitative research. Whether the outcome of the research will be statistics or an in-depth analysis of a market, the way the research is carried out must be valid, reliable and representative.

3.6.1 Valid research

To ensure that research results are valid it is important to collect the right information. Deciding on what the right information is demands some expertise and knowledge of the marketplace. Market researchers have to devise research that will give as accurate a picture as possible of the preferences of the potential market.

The success or failure of new products is determined not only by the merits of the products themselves but also by a host of other factors. For example a company that has previously made products for sale at the budget end of the market may not succeed with the launch of a luxury item. In such a situation a good product could potentially fail because the company or brand name has been associated with low-cost or poor-quality products in the past. To inform the marketing strategy in such a case the researchers would have to devise research to look not only at reactions to the product itself but also at consumer attitudes towards the company and its competitors. This would enable the company to ascertain whether or not this new venture is viable.

3.6.2 Reliable research

To conduct reliable research it is important to ensure there is no bias in the way that questions are asked or the tests carried out. An example from the food industry is that of soft-drinks producer Pepsi, which carried out taste tests of a new drink against its rival Coca Cola. Pepsi had its drink in a container labelled 'M' and Coca Cola in a container labelled 'Q'. Pepsi came out best in every test. It was later discovered by Coca Cola that respondents have a tendency to prefer containers labelled 'M' over those labelled 'Q' regardless of their contents – Coca Cola found this out by putting the same drink in both containers.

Qualitative research requires the researchers to ask probing questions without leading the interviewees in a particular direction or putting words into their mouths.

3.6.3 Representative research

To make sure that research results are representative of the potential market, the sample of consumers chosen must represent the characteristics of that market. For example a company wanting to research the market for a new vacuum cleaner may define its target market by income brackets and ages. Researchers would then have to devise a way of finding a representative sample of potential purchasers to question about their requirements. This would mean finding the right proportions of women, men, ages, incomes, occupational backgrounds, and so forth.

Even qualitative research requires respondents to be representative of a target market. Although the numbers of respondents in a qualitative survey may be statistically insignificant, the right kinds of respondents still have to be found. For example to find out about the needs of housebound elderly users it would be more appropriate to go to a sheltered housing complex to find respondents, rather than to look for elderly people in an out-of-town shopping centre.

3.6.4 Using samples

Because it is impossible to interview every potential customer, all market research must rely on a sample of the population being surveyed, interviewed or tested. There are two kinds of sampling.

Probability sampling employs scientific rules to ensure the sample chosen is representative. Every individual in the population has a known chance of being selected. For example researchers may choose potential respondents at random from a list of all of the business customers of the manufacturing company commissioning the research.

Non-probability sampling is a less expensive alternative, which relies on the researchers' judgement to choose the respondents. Non-probability sampling is used where a representative sample is less important. For example in the early stages of product development a small number of potential customers might be approached for their views on several concepts, with the aim of eliminating the least favoured ones.

3.6.5 Market research steps

For any piece of market research the steps that will be followed will be the same, regardless of the techniques used.

Step 1 Define

Before starting the research the problem or area of research needs to be well defined and the objectives of the research thought out. In other words, what do you need to know and what do you want to get out of your research?

Step 2 Plan

Next a plan for collecting the information needed has to be drawn up and the methods and sources to be used have to be identified. In other words, who are you going to collect information from and how do you plan to do this?

Step 3 Research

Then the research has to be carried out and the information collected.

Step 4 Analyse

Importantly the information collected has to be analysed and evaluated and its implications thought about. Some research techniques require more formal analysis than others do but all require reflection on the results that have been collected. In other words, what does this mean and what are the most important points to come out of this?

Step 5 Report

Finally the results of the research have to be written up in the form of a report. In order to make findings available to a wide audience the results of any research need to be written so that the information can be disseminated and acted upon.

Project

You will find it useful to remind yourself of these steps when you are working on the project for this course. You should also read the description of market research techniques that follows, with a view to selecting appropriate techniques to help you to gather ideas and information for your project work.

3.7 How researchers find out about markets

There are many different techniques for researching the market. Researchers have to choose the methods that are most appropriate to the market sector and the type of product being launched. Their starting point will almost always be an examination of the trends in the market environment, as I discussed when looking at marketing decision support systems. Examination of the market environment sets the context for primary market research, identifying who and what needs to be asked.

3.7.1 Surveys

One of the most frequently used methods for data collection in the consumer sector is the survey (see Box 2). Surveys may also be used in other sectors, although the respondents to the surveys may be companies rather than individuals. There are many forms of survey, with levels of contact going from personal to impersonal.

most personal

- personal interviews
  - group interviews
    - telephone interviews
      - internet surveys
        - postal questionnaires
          - point-of-sale data collection

          least personal

Box 2   Good and bad surveys

Most people have experience of answering survey questions but if you are designing your own survey it is important to think hard about what you need to know, before you start writing your questions. If you have taken surveys in the past that have asked you to indicate your income level, you may think that you have to put a question of this sort on a survey for it to be valid.

> Indicate below the level of income for your entire household for one year:
>
> (a) less than £10 000
>
> (b) £10 000 to £19 999
>
> (c) £20 000 to £29 999
>
> (d) £30 000 to £39 999
>
> (e) £40 000 to £49 999
>
> (f) £50 000 to £70 000
>
> (g) more than £70 000

What would the answers to this question tell you?

This information could help you to put some of the answers to other questions that you have asked into context. For example if you also asked how many times the respondent has been on holiday in the past year you may see a correlation between income and the number of times they have been away. Information of this nature is most useful when planning a targeted sales campaign. If you are constructing a survey to find information that may help you to develop a new product, your need is more likely to be for information about attitudes to existing products or problem situations. For example:

> How do you find setting your DVD player to record a programme?
>
> (a) very easy
>
> (b) quite easy
>
> (c) neither easy nor difficult
>
> (d) quite difficult
>
> (e) very difficult

Another way of presenting the same question might be as follows:

> How easy do you find it to set your DVD player to record a programme? Indicate on the scale below:
>
> very easy   1   2   3   4   5   very difficult

The way questions are asked can affect the response that you get. Think about the question I have asked above. If I had asked 'How difficult do you find it to set your DVD player?', there is an implication in the question that setting the DVD player is a difficult thing to do. Where possible, a neutral question will elicit a more accurate response than a question that is biased.

To inform new product development, I would expect a questionnaire containing a question like the one above to ask further questions to find out more about the problem – for example rating the ease of use of the remote control, the menu system, the onscreen information and so on.

One question that I have often seen on student surveys reads something like this:

How much would you be prepared to pay for a product that solves all of the problems above?

(a) less than £5

(b) £5–10

(c) £10–15

(d) £15–20

(e) more than £20

There are several problems with this question.

Firstly it usually follows a number of questions that may bias the respondent towards indicating that they have a problem with something that they had not previously regarded as an issue. Coming at the end of this series of questions, the respondent is unlikely to want to displease the surveyor by answering that they would not buy the product, even if this were to be offered as an option.

Secondly it is hard for people to say realistically how much they would pay for a product that only exists as a solution concept.

Thirdly it may only be possible to make the proposed product at a cost higher than any of the respondents have indicated. Although this question would give the surveyor some indication that the market may not be willing to pay for the product at a realistic price, it may be more useful to have a good idea about potential production costs before carrying out such market research.

This kind of question may be much better dealt with by using other techniques, such as focus groups or interviews, where the respondent could be given more detail or asked more probing questions that would give a truer indication of their response to the potential new product.

3.7.2 Personal interviews

Interviews can be conducted in a number of ways. They may be with individuals or groups; and they may be *in-depth* or *short*. There are three types of interview used in research.

- *Structured* interviews involve the interviewer having a set list of questions with a range of possible answers to be ticked off as appropriate.

- *Semi-structured* interviews may use a checklist of topics to be covered but allow the interviewees to respond in their own way to prompts from the interviewer.

- *Non-directive* interviews are interviews in which the interviewees are invited to talk about a topic or product with no specific questions being asked. The interviewer in that situation helps the discussion along.

The correlation of these is shown in Table 4.

Table 4   Types of interview with individuals and groups

	Structured	Semi-structured	Non-directive
Individual	in-depth or short	in-depth or short	in-depth or short
Group	in-depth or short	in-depth or short	in-depth or short

The location where interviews are carried out will vary from situation to situation. Some short, structured interviews will be carried out in the street, or at a trade show. You will probably have seen, if not been interviewed by, market researchers with clipboards. However non-directive interviews are more likely to be carried out in an individual's home, on a company's premises or in a venue set up for the occasion, such as a conference centre or hotel meeting room. The reasons should be obvious: the researcher carrying out the interview wants the interviewee to focus on the question and think about their answers.

Handling the data collected

The less structured the interview, the more complicated the analysis of the information becomes and the more the researcher has to make judgements about the data.

Although the outcome of non-directive interviews provides a challenge when it comes to analysing the data, these interviews may elicit valuable and unexpected information. This makes this form of interviewing particularly valuable when developing ideas for innovations and concepts for new product development.

Semi-structured or non-directive in-depth interviews are valuable when trying to develop an understanding of the market, whereas shorter structured interviews may help researchers to gather answers to specific questions of preference or attitude.

One criticism of in-depth interviews is that they may be highly subjective, especially when techniques have been used to obtain information about the subconscious motives of the respondent.

Exercise 8   Interview approaches

Match the three questions below to the different interview approaches of structured, semi-structured and non-directive. Which of these approaches are qualitative and which are quantitative?

1   Can you describe briefly how you write assignments?

2   Which of the following do you use to write assignments?

   (a) pen

   (b) computer

   (c) typewriter

   (d) none of these.

3   Tell me about your OU studies.

Discussion

Question 1 is an example of a semi-structured question. The respondent is given some guidance as to how much to say ('describe briefly') and what to talk about. The interviewer may be working from a checklist or a set list of questions. If the interviewee starts rambling off the point, the interviewer will try to get the interview back on track by picking up points or asking further questions. This approach is qualitative.

Question 2 is an example of a structured question. The possible responses are limited. The person constructing the questions must have considered all of the likely and possible options and written them down. The questions asked will depend on what they want to find out. A failure to predict responses correctly and provide respondents with a good choice can lead to data that is misleading or inaccurate. A few well-constructed questions may find out more than sheets and sheets of questions that provide information that is not important or relevant. This approach is quantitative.

Question 3 is an example of a non-directive question. The respondent is given free rein to talk about their experience as they wish. The interviewer may pick up on comments the interviewee makes and ask them to say more about that topic or clarify what they mean, but the lead comes from the interviewee rather than the interviewer. This approach is qualitative.

3.7.3 Hall tests

Hall tests, sometimes referred to as face-value tests, are a way of seeking formal, quantitative information about reactions to new products, using personal interviewing. A number of products are displayed in a local hall – hence the term – and members of the public are invited to evaluate the products on show. These products may be only from the manufacturer conducting the research or might include competitors' products. Often the brand name and identifying features will be concealed, to avoid bias. The company takes its products, and possibly those of the competition, to halls or shopping centres around the country. In the USA these tests are known as mall tests because they take place in shopping malls.

At each site, people are chosen from among passers by so that a range of ages, socio-economic classes and incomes are represented. The chosen individuals look at the products and fill in a questionnaire to evaluate and rank various features of the products on display. The questionnaire may also be designed to gather some information about what would motivate them to buy the products on display. Participants are often offered a small incentive for giving their time to take part in this exercise.

Hall tests enable a relatively large number of respondents to be screened and contacted. Interviews can be carried out in reasonably controlled conditions. The technique is a useful way of reaching a large sample of people quickly. Some researchers use hall tests as a way of finding a few respondents for more in-depth interviews.

3.7.4 Group interviews

Focus groups

Group interviews can be useful for obtaining feedback and ideas. The dynamics of the group may bring to light issues or attitudes that would not emerge if each of the members of the group were to be interviewed individually. A well-known and well-used form of group interview is the focus group. Focus groups have been used extensively, not just to research products but also to research attitudes towards politicians and government initiatives.

Focus groups can be used to obtain reactions to a product idea or even a prototype product, but they are also extensively used in some industries to obtain comments on proposed advertising campaigns and marketing strategies. Focus groups can be a useful way of developing and testing ideas for innovative product concepts.

The focus group may contain a range of people who represent identified market segments – such as different ages and ethnicity – or it may comprise people who are all from the same market segment, for example a group of young people who are interested in music. The group is led by a trained moderator, who focuses the participants on the topic in an open-ended discussion.

Projective techniques

Sometimes instead of straight questions, techniques are used to help researchers to understand attitudes or motivations. Projective techniques are one such approach. Like many market research techniques, these techniques draw upon the science of psychology, and particularly on psychodynamic theories. There are many variants of projective techniques but they all share the characteristic of presenting respondents with a scenario in the form of a picture or a set of words and asking for their response.

These techniques are particularly useful when the information sought is personal. People are more likely to project their true feelings onto the given situation than to reveal such personal information under direct questioning.

Below are some variants of the projective techniques.

Sentence completion

Respondents are given incomplete sentences and asked to complete them. These sentences are about someone else and are deliberately ambiguous so that the response reveals something of the interviewee's personality and attitudes. The skill in using this technique lies in finding a prompt that elicits an honest response, rather than a flippant or misleading response.

For example:

- 'Sustainable design is about...'
- 'In the sustainable future, I wish...'

Word association

This technique can be used in different ways:

- randomly feeding respondents words or phrases and asking them to tell you the word or phrase that comes into their heads
- asking respondents what words come into their heads when certain brand names are mentioned
- asking respondents to respond to advertising slogans
- asking respondents to describe an object or product using metaphors, human or animal characteristics, or adjectives – for example, 'If this computer were a person, what music would it like?'.

The skill in this technique is in finding sets of words that will generate meaningful responses that can be analysed and used.

Thematic apperception tests

Thematic apperception tests are also known as the picture interpretation technique. These tests involve showing respondents a picture or sequence of pictures and asking them to describe what is happening, what is being said or what happens next (Figure 22). The skill with this technique is in providing a picture that provokes discussion but that is open to interpretation so that respondents are not led to particular conclusions and do not guess what the research is trying to find out.

This technique can be used to find out a range of things, from the qualities associated with products to perceptions of the people who use certain products or services.

Figure 22 A photo such as this may be shown as part of a thematic apperception test Source: Getty Images

Third-person technique

This technique, more than any other, is used to find out how people feel and to coax opinions that might be seen as negative. The respondents are asked questions about someone else – it may be someone they know, such as a relative or neighbour. The aim of this technique is to encourage them to talk about attitudes they might not admit to holding themselves. For example the interviewer might ask, 'What would you think if your neighbour bought this car?' The interviewee will reveal more about their feelings than if simply asked, 'What do you think about this car?'.

Sometimes this technique is used with role-play so that the interviewees act out how the other person would respond. This can be particularly helpful when trying to find out how children feel about products, as they can express emotions even if they find it hard to discuss in the abstract.

This technique requires skilful interpretation and analysis of the responses that are received.

The information gained from focus groups and projective techniques is qualitative. The number of people involved (sample size) is small and the data collected consists of subjective information about feelings, preferences and perceptions that cannot easily be quantified. There are, however, some established research techniques whereby researchers have direct contact with groups of people, and for which the results can be more readily quantified. One such technique is the use of panels, which is discussed below.

3.7.5 Panels

For some products it is useful to the researcher to gather data about a product or service over time. In such situations researchers may put together a panel of users who will be asked to report on their experience at regular intervals. Research into users' developing opinions in this way is often used at the pilot stage of new product development.

Alternatively panels of users may be created as a reference group and their opinions canvassed on a number of different topics, on a regular basis. For example panel members may receive a postal questionnaire on alternate weeks and attend focus groups monthly. Panel members receive financial incentives for this participation.

In the UK the Consumers' Association uses panels to assess and report on users' experiences of different products. The research carried out in this way can be either quantitative or qualitative depending on the research techniques used with panel members. The Consumers' Association panel has over 1000 members, whose interests and life situations are used to select suitable participants for surveys and user trials appropriately.

The testing house that carries out some of the research for the Consumers' Association, ETL Semko, can be seen on the T307 DVD. This testing house also has its own panel of 500 members, used for research for manufacturers, as well as a specialist panel of 250 disabled people.

3.7.6 Telephone interviewing

Telephone interviews can be an effective way of making contact with respondents and conducting short interviews that do not require any visual stimulus. The phone interview allows the quick gathering of information over any geographical distance and is as flexible as a personal interview, at a much lower cost. An experienced interviewer with a good script can interview up to 50 respondents a day.

The disadvantages are that non-phone owners are excluded from the research and that some people are reluctant to disclose certain information over the phone. However this remains a popular survey method.

Web-assisted telephone interviewing

Recent developments in technology mean that some researchers are now using *web-assisted* telephone interviewing. This technique combines use of the internet with telephone interviews and is used when the respondent needs to be shown visual stimulus material.

This technique is used mainly for gathering quantitative data on such things as responses to advertising and perceptions of brands.

Potential interviewees are identified and telephoned, to make an appointment for the interview. At the start of the interview the interviewee is asked to log onto a website containing the visual material. The researcher then talks the interviewee through the set questions over the phone.

3.7.7 Observation

The technique of observation derives originally from the social science of anthropology and is frequently used by marketing professionals. However this form of market research is one that is also adopted by designers themselves, as will be discussed in Section 5. As you might imagine, observation techniques involve the researcher observing potential purchasers or users handling or using products, or making purchasing decisions.

The way observation is carried out may be structured or unstructured. An example of structured observation might be looking for a specific behaviour and ticking this off on a checklist when seen. Unstructured observation might entail observing purchasers while using a product, and recording this behaviour in detail.

This technique can be a good stimulus for ideas. For example the idea for sticking plasters with pictures on them came from the observation that children were drawing on their plasters. Toy manufacturers such as Lego and Fisher Price regularly observe children playing with their products, as a form of market testing of new products and idea generation.

3.7.8 Techniques with no personal contact

Sometimes researchers choose techniques involving no personal contact between researcher and respondent. Such techniques are often the least expensive way to gather information over a wide geographical area. The main techniques are questionnaires delivered by post or electronic means and continuous data collection methods.

Postal surveys

Surveys by mail generally have a low response rate and are relatively time consuming in terms of gathering data, compared with other, more direct interviewing techniques. One return for every 10 questionnaires sent out is considered to be a good rate of return. However postal surveys are relatively inexpensive to conduct and can cover wide geographical areas and large samples.

The questionnaires have to be well structured and clear if any useful information is to be obtained from them. Pilot testing of questionnaires is essential before a large mail-shot. The disadvantages are that the data cannot be queried or probed, and there may be bias because the respondents are self-selected. Much of the information gathered in this way is used to inform marketing campaigns or to sound out potential purchasers so that promotional materials can be sent to the people most likely to respond positively.

Omnibus surveys

In addition to surveys about individual products, there are also omnibus surveys. These are surveys of consumer purchasing behaviour, financed by many different companies subscribing to the survey. These companies contribute their own questions, and only receive the responses to these questions.

Market research companies frequently conduct postal surveys on behalf of a number of interested businesses. Often an incentive is offered for filling in lengthy questionnaires, and a pen is sometimes provided to prompt potential respondents to answer as soon as they open the envelope. Do the incentives and pens encourage you to fill in such surveys?

Internet surveys

Internet surveys have become increasingly important since the 1990s. Cheaper than postal surveys they also have the advantage that the responses are collected in electronic form. This enables the results to be processed immediately and respondents may even be able to see how their responses compare with those of other respondents.

Internet surveys usually ask structured questions. Respondents are asked to select their responses by clicking on a button next to the answer that is most appropriate. However as web technologies have developed, some internet surveys now include more visual questions to elicit responses to advertisements or packaging design. Respondents may even be asked for qualitative responses.

The limitation of internet surveys is fairly obvious – they can only be administered to internet users, which excludes some groups.

As with postal surveys, incentives may sometimes be offered to respondents, such as a earning points that can be exchanged for goods or entering the respondent in a sweepstake.

The results of a poll in Figure 23 give an idea of how survey data can be presented.

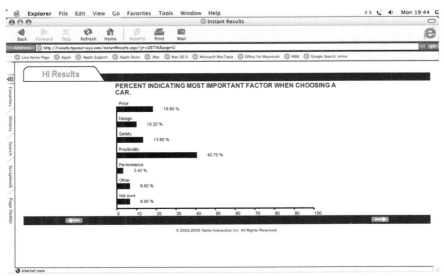

Figure 23 Results of an internet survey Source: Harris Poll Online

Unlike a postal survey, where respondents may choose not to answer questions, the software used for the internet survey can be programmed to prompt respondents if they fail to respond to a particular question or if they select too many or too few options for a question. The survey can also be tailored to the responses, so if for example the respondent answers 'No' to the question 'Do you have a pet?', they will not then be required to answer more detailed questions about their pet and its care. This, and the presentation of a few questions at a time, rather than a lengthy printed document, can make internet surveys more attractive than their postal equivalent.

A perceived disadvantage may be the cost of being online to fill in the survey, although the spread of broadband and networks in the workplace have made this less of a problem for many potential respondents.

Point-of-sale data collection

Point-of-sale information involves information about sales being collected on a regular basis from sales outlets. This is known as *continuous data collection*. The collection of such information focuses on either sales of particular products or the purchasing behaviour of identified consumer groups. There are a number of different ways this type of information can be collected.

Retail audits

Retail audits focus on how well particular products are selling. They are conducted by monitoring the sales from a fixed sample of shops to provide information about the sales and pricing. Such audits allow comparison of the sales from different sorts of outlets, as well as indicating regional variations in sales patterns.

Electronic panels

By contrast, consumer scanner panels focus on the buying habits of identified groups of consumers. This is an electronic variant of the customer panels discussed earlier. Loyalty cards, such as the Tesco Clubcard, issued by retailers to customers enable electronic monitoring of purchasing decisions simply by swiping or punching the consumer's card at the supermarket checkout. This enables purchases to be associated with the demographic and purchase characteristics of individual consumers. Researchers using this technique may select consumers with particular characteristics and look closely at their purchases over time.

3.8   Perceptual mapping

Many market research techniques aim to better understand consumers. The techniques of perceptual mapping are concerned with consumer perceptions rather than consumer behaviour. Perceptual mapping techniques are often used to compare products – you have probably seen techniques of this kind being used in postal and internet surveys. Box 3 outlines two mapping techniques: *Likert scales* and *semantic differential scales*.

Box 3   Perceptual mapping techniques

Likert scales

Likert (pronounced lick-ert) scales are widely used to measure attitudes in many arenas, not only in product development. There is a strong possibility that at some point in your life you have been asked to fill in a Likert scale to give your opinion on something.

The basis of this technique is that respondents are presented with a series of statements and asked to score each of these using a five-point scale:

1   agree strongly

2   agree slightly

3   neither agree nor disagree

4   disagree slightly

5   disagree strongly.

For example:

A personal music player is a fashion accessory

1	2	3	4	5

1 = agree strongly; 5 = disagree strongly

The procedure for drawing up a Likert scale is to start with in-depth and semi-structured interviewing and use the outcomes of these interviews to generate a list of statements. The first draft of the Likert scale is then tested on a sample of about 100 users before being sent to the full-sized sample.

A variation on this technique is sometime used in which, rather than agreeing or disagreeing, respondents are asked to rank using other criteria, for example helpfulness and importance.

Semantic differential scales

Semantic differential scales are used to find out how people think about products. Similarly to the Likert scale, the starting point for the research is to carry out in-depth interviews with potential users. These interviews are used to help the researcher understand and generate the *constructs* that people have when thinking about a given product or service. Mental constructs are the ideas and theories that affect the ways people view and understand the world around them.

The constructs generated are then used to develop an attitude battery, which allows researchers to find out how products are perceived by a greater number of people. For each construct, respondents are invited to rate a product on a scale between the two opposing expressions of that construct (see Figure 24).

Respondents may be asked to rate a product against 20 different constructs on a page. In addition they may be asked to show how their ideal product would rate or they may be required to carry out the exercise for competing products. When the attitude battery is complete there will be a profile of each user's responses to enable comparisons.

When an attitude battery is used to collect data about a number of different brands the data can be mapped by computer to show how competing products relate to one another in the user's mind. (See Figure 24.) This may lead to surprising insights for the manufacturer. For example a perceptual mapping exercise on food found the nearest competitor to lamb chops was fish fingers.

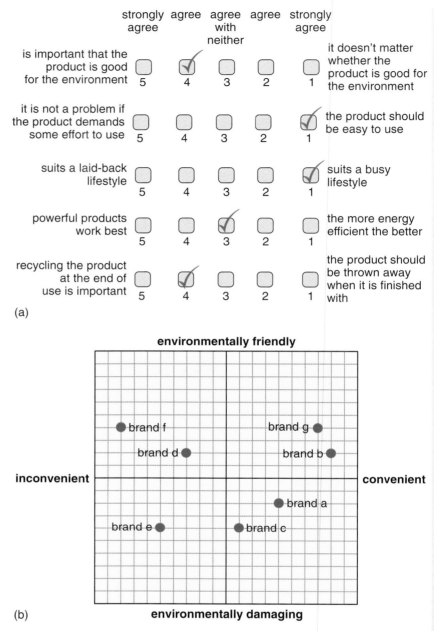

(a)

(b)

Figure 24 (a) Attitude battery with boxes ticked to show choices made. (b) Results of an attitude battery for brands a to g mapped on to a perceptual map where the constructs used are environmental impact and convenience.

Designers at Philips Design used a semantic differential scale (Figure 25) in conjunction with cultural probe techniques (described later) to explore how a group of technologically aware young people viewed their world. This group was called 'plugged-ins' by the designers, to denote how the young people used both information and communication technologies and developed an awareness of trends in music. This research led designers to a better understanding of the use of music as a form of self-expression and inspired them to design a product concept that brought together music, visual display and clothing.

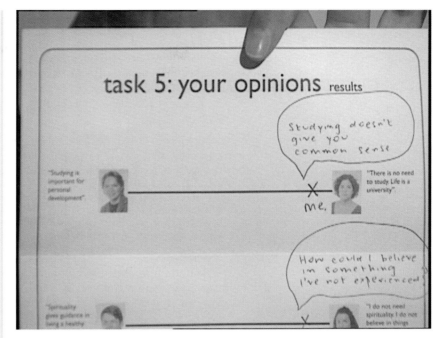

Figure 25   Part of a semantic differential scale. This scale is about studying and the top handwritten note says, 'Studying doesn't give you common sense'.

SAQ 11

Draw up a table to show which of the techniques discussed in this section are qualitative and which are quantitative.

SAQ 12

Which techniques are most useful for finding out about established products and planning incremental innovations?

SAQ 13

Which techniques are most useful for planning and testing radically new products and technical innovations?

Exercise 9   Approaches to market research

Now read the article below by Bettina von Stamm about the use of market research as a tool for innovators. I have not introduced all of the market research techniques that she mentions but the text is printed in its entirety so that you can follow her argument.

You will see that there are limitations to conventional market research when working on highly innovative projects. As you read, think of some of the innovations you have read about so far and consider whether the arguments von Stamm makes apply to them.

Approaches to market research

Bettina von Stamm

Market research tends to be an important part in a company's armoury to develop and verify new products and services. Not least because best-practice literature has shouted for years about how important it is to meet consumer needs for a product to be successful. Most companies translated this into the need to conduct market research and involve consumers throughout the development process. However, what managers need to be careful about is what kind of approach to market research they take and how much they let results influence their decisions. In the case of Black & Decker, should the market research data available dictate which design to take forward? Rather the devil you know.

Particularly in the context of innovation, there is a considerable problem with market research: if you ask people what they want, they will refer to something they are familiar with. Kaplan comments,

> Customers seldom articulate needs they don't know they have. Ten years ago, how many people would have asked for a subscription to anything like America Online? Thirty years ago, how many people would have asked for a calculator that fits into a shirt pocket – or a microwave, or a VCR, or a Walkman?

So it is important to understand the limitations of market research, and more importantly, to understand the need to match the approach taken to market research with the development aim in mind.

There are two main different approaches, quantitative and qualitative. The former involves surveys and questionnaires, the latter interviews, focus groups and observations. After some general insights on market research, this chapter looks at traditional market research methods and the most recent developments.

What is it about market research?

Research with members of the Innovation Exchange revealed that most companies are dissatisfied with the results of current market research practices. Taking a closer look at how many companies conduct their research gives an indication why, more often than not, the activity is outsourced to an external agency. This means the information the company gets back has been filtered through the market research agency's lenses, or as a member of the innovation exchange put it, 'You generally only get a summary of the research but researchers do not necessarily have the knowledge and understanding of the market to interpret the results "correctly"'. As Bobrow (1997) recommends in his book *Complete Idiots Guide to New Product Development*, 'Use it [market research]. Don't believe it.' You may have already heard the following story that illustrates this point.

A car manufacturer, just having finished a prototype of its new small car, commissioned a market research agency to find out what consumers would think about it. When the research report came back the engineers were surprised to read that customers were not quite happy with the engine performance. It was only a small car and the engine was already quite powerful. But still, give the consumer what the consumer wants. So the engineers reworked the engine, and the revised model was market tested again. But still, the results said that consumers wanted more power. This circle was repeated a few times until the engineers threw their hands up and said, 'This cannot be true! Let's speak to the researchers or even better, be present when they conduct their research.' And indeed, a good idea it was. When the engineers were present and could actually observe the consumer and talk to them directly they realized that not the real power of the engine but the perceived power was the issue. What consumers were missing was the feeling of gently being pushed back into the seat when accelerating – something that could be fixed easily – and quickly as well as cheaply – by changing the upholstery.

This story illustrates clearly it is not about getting data, but interpreting the feedback correctly and applying insights and expertise to come to the right conclusions, extracting meaning from the data, converting it into information. When selecting a particular method for a piece of market research, the two critical questions are, will this type of research be able to collect the data we need, and will the way the data is treated maximize its value?

Another issue with market research is that it is often undertaken to confirm results or beliefs, rather than to gain new insights. Market research is sometimes commissioned with the aim of generating some 'ammunition' to help sell a particular concept – and when the answers are not as desired, they often get ignored.

But even if market research is taken seriously and conducted appropriately, the results are not necessarily a good indicator for what is going to happen upon the introduction of the product. Let me just give you a couple of examples.

- 190 000 consumers testing the New Coke against the existing formula overwhelmingly declared that they preferred the new taste, but its launch was a failure (Martin, 1995).

- In consumer research, McDonald's found that consumers wanted healthier burgers – but when they launched their diet burger, McLean, it was a flop. People continued to buy the nice fatty, greasy burger (Martin, 1995).

If market research does not seem to be a good predictor for market success, its predictive power of market failure is similarly (un)impressive. Kaplan (1999) reports, 'When tested through market research, the HP35 calculator, the first videocassette recorder, the fax machine and Federal Express all received negative ratings!' or as another story from Martin's article shows:

> When Compaq first thought about Systempro, PC-based servers, everyone in the industry declared that this surely, was beyond personal computers and had to be done on a mainframe. Gary Stimac, then Compaq's senior vice president who led the team recalls, 'By the end of 1990, Systempro's first year in the market, it generated only $200m in revenue. But we did not give up and continued to educate the market. It typically takes 12–18 months to get good read on whether what you are hearing is surmountable scepticism or a downright lack of market acceptance.' In 1994 Compaq sold $1.8bn worth of Systempro, equalling 17 per cent of the company's revenue.

These insights – failure of current market research practices to deliver accurate results and the problems of misinterpretation through external research agencies – lead companies to reconsider their approach. Involving people from within the organization in market research exercises is a possible solution, as a quote from a government website on best practice in service acquisition illustrates.

In the past, it was not unusual for technical staff to conduct market research about marketplace offerings, while contracting staff conducted market research more focused on industry practices and pricing. A better approach is for the entire integrated solutions team to be a part of the market research effort. This enables the members of the team to share an understanding and knowledge of the marketplace – an important factor in the development of the acquisition strategy – and a common understanding of what features, schedules, terms and conditions are key.

Another is to send out your staff to observe your product or service in action.

> The starting point for innovation is to connect with the consumer. This has been a weakness over the past 4–5 years; we were too removed from the consumers. We are now asking our people to go and talk to consumers where they spend their lives – in bars, sports fields, shopping centres – to find out how they actually live. We can already see that when we understand the consumer more we have great success.
>
> (interview with a manager from an Innovation Exchange member company)

Another good source for customer insights many organizations ignore are the front-line sales people. They have direct contact and can often observe the customer using the product. However, mechanisms need to be put in place to ensure that the feedback that comes from the front line is honest and straight. Most sales people are not motivated to feed back if there are any 'problems', nor are they rewarded for ideas, they are rewarded for sales. This may also influence their listening ability: they listen to sell, not to learn. Companies can improve the process by putting systems in place that encourage sales staff to feed back any useful information, e.g. introduce customer visit feedback forms and ensure that rewards are not counterproductive – but don't forget to train the sales people so they know what they are expected to do and look out for.

Traditional approaches to market research

Keeping the above in mind, what are approaches to market research? Traditional approaches to market research all have one thing in common, they are based on asking the consumer what he or she wants, through the collection of either quantitative or qualitative data. Under the category of quantitative research we find different distribution methods of surveys and questionnaire: per mail, over the telephone, in person, either in home or office, or 'on the street' and more recently, via email or on the internet.

The three main qualitative market research methods are interviews, focus groups and observation – or in fact, a combination. Qualitative approaches have the advantage that they generate a deeper level of understanding of consumer needs and viewpoints. However, artefacts such as drawings, prototypes, or the finished product can be used for either. As mentioned before it is horses for courses. Table 9.1 by Steven Cohen (1996) compares methods of quantitative market research, whereby the last two columns also shed some light on the benefits of qualitative interviewing.

But there are not only different approaches to consider; managers should also think about during which stages of the development process they seek to involve consumers. Bruce and Copper (1997, p86) suggest that market research has a part to play in all stages of market development. Conveniently, Mahajan and Wind (1992) provide a matrix with different approaches to market research on one axis and different new product development stages on the other, suggesting which approach is appropriate for what stage (see Table 9.2).

Another question is how many people to ask to get some meaningful insights? Cohen (1996) has collected data that provides some guidelines on typical sample sizes for different types of quantitative marketing research studies (Table 9.3).

Table 9.1 Comparing approaches to market research

	Survey method			
	Mail	Telephone	In person (home or office)	In person (intercept)
Use of incentives	recommended	not necessary except in rare cases	recommended	recommended
Cost per interview	low	depends on population to be reached	high	moderate
Ability to use visuals and physical prototypes or do taste tests	visuals only	not possible	yes	no
Possible interview complexity	few skip patterns, many complex question types possible	complex skip patterns, many question types not possible	both complex skip patterns and question types are possible	both complex skip patterns and question types are possible
Awareness, open-ended questions, and probes	not possible	possible	possible	possible
Speed of response	slow	fast	moderate	moderate
Security	low	high	moderate	high
Survey length	long surveys possible	moderate length	long surveys possible	long surveys possible
Control over who responds	low	high	high	high
Control over conduct of interviews	low	high	moderate	high

Source: Cohen, 1996

The reliability of the data will vary from industry to industry, and with varying user groups. For example, research that involves professional users and buyers tends to be much more reliable than research undertaken with consumers stopped in the street, and insights from research for fast-moving consumer goods (FMCGs) tend to be more reliable than those from research regarding capital expenditure goods.

The future

Given that traditional approaches to market research do not seem to work too well, particularly in the context of innovation, what then are approaches that might help? Sanchez and Sudharshan (1993) recommend what they call 'real-time market research'. In their words, real-time market research involves, 'To offer batches of actual new product models to consumers to learn their exact and varied preferences as to alternative product configurations, features and performance levels.' This approach, so they claim, overcomes some of the limitations and time requirements of traditional market research methods – for a list of what Mahajan and Wind (1992) consider to be the major shortcomings see Table 9.4.

Table 9.2 Use of models and methods of market research across new product development activities

	Focus group	Limited rollout	Concept tests	Show test/clinic	Attitude, usage studies	Conjoint analysis	Delphi panel	Quality function deployment	Home usage test	Product life-cycle models	Synectics
New product idea generation	X	X	X				X	X		X	X
New product screening	X	X	X	X	X	X	X				
Market study for concept development	X	X	X	X	X						X
Market identification positioning, marketing strategy specification	X	X	X		X	X		X		X	
Business/finance analysis			X		X	X				X	
Product development		X	X	X		X		X	X		
Consumer test of products	X	X	X	X		X			X		
Pre-market volume forecasting				X		X					
Market test/trial sell		X		X							
Market launch planning	X	X	X	X	X					X	

Source: Mahajan and Wind, 1992

Table 9.3 Sample size for market research studies

Study	Minimum size	Typical size (range)
Market studies	500	1000–1500
Strategic studies	200	400–500
Test market penetration studies	200	300–500
Concept/product tests	200	200–300/cell
Name tests	100/name variant	200–300/cell
Package tests	100/package variant	200–300/cell
TV, radio commercial tests	150/commercial	200–300/commercial
Print add tests	150/advertisement	200–300/commercial

Source: Cohen, 1996

Table 9.4 Traditional models of market research and their shortcomings

Models	Major shortcomings
Focus group	market complexity not captured
Limited rollout	too much time to implement
Concept tests	forecast inaccuracy
Show test/clinic	too much time to implement
Attitude, usage studies	forecast inaccuracy
Conjoint analysis (1)	expensive; complexity not captured
Delphi panel (2)	market complexity not captured
Quality function deployment (3)	forecast inaccuracy; too much time
Home usage test	expensive; too much time
Product life-cycle models	forecast inaccuracy
Synectics (4)	expensive; forecast inaccuracy

(1) Bobrow (1997) describes conjoint analysis as 'a technique for separating and measuring respondents' judgements about complex alternatives, usually product characteristics or attributes, into distinct components'.
(2) Delphi technique – elicits ideas from participants by means of a series of highly structured and progressively more focused questionnaires; initial questionnaire is sent out, questions are summarized and rephrased into a new set of questions which is re-sent to initial participants; process is repeated.
(3) Quality function deployment (QFD) – a matrix with product characteristics and attributes on the one axis and customers needs on the other is used to determine where to focus development efforts.
(4) Synectics is not necessarily classified as a tool for market research. It can be described as a structured team approach to problem solving and idea generation, promoted originally by a company of the same name.
Source: Mahajan and Wind, 1992

However, real-time market research does not really overcome the problem of people knowing what they like and liking what they know. There are two possible ways of addressing this issue. The first is, if innovative products or ideas are concerned, work with a group of people who are known to like change and new things, don't work with traditionalists who always prefer the 'good old days'. Find the 'Vorreiter', the pioneers of new products and technologies who like nothing better than a new toy. They are more likely to be open and positive towards new things. The most leading-edge market research and launch strategists go even further; rather than launching a product or service and leaving it to advertising and other sales-enhancing techniques to establish the product in the marketplace, they aim to identify trend leaders and let them promote the product instead. If the right people can be identified, marketers can achieve a market pull – instead of the company push – for their innovation, an approach called 'viral marketing'. The art lies in identifying who the right people to create a market are. However, it is also expensive.

The second way is not to ask people what they want, but observe what they actually do. This approach is particularly useful at the idea generation stage, as it helps to identify latent consumer needs – those needs of which the consumers might not even be aware – but if you are able to identify such a need, and develop a solution for it, you are on to a winner. One company well known for this approach is IDEO (www.ideo.com).

Harvard academics Leonard and Rayport (1997) called this approach 'empathic design'. They explain,

> Empathic design calls for company representatives to watch customers using products and services in the context of their own environments. By doing so, managers can often identify unexpected uses for their products. They can also uncover problems that customers do not mention in surveys.

Companies can engage in empathic design, or similar techniques such as contextual inquiry, in a variety of ways. However, most employ the following 5-step process:

1 observation

2 capturing data

3 reflection and analysis

4 brainstorming for solutions

5 developing prototypes of possible solutions.

In Table 9.5, Leonard and Rayport contrast the traditional approach of asking people what they want with the observation approach.

It is approaches such as 'empathic design' and 'infectious marketing' that are more likely to identify seed for innovations than market research methods that count 'ticks in a box' and rely on statistical analysis.

Table 9.5 Comparing the traditional approach with empathic design

Inquiry	Observation
people can't ask for what they don't know is technically possible	well-chosen observers have deep knowledge of corporate capabilities, including the extent of the company's technical expertise
people are generally highly unreliable reporters of their own behaviour	observers rely on real actions rather than reported behaviour
people tend to give answers they think are expected or desired	people are not asked to respond to verbal stimuli, they give nonverbal cues of their feelings and responses through body language, in addition to spontaneous, unsolicited comments
people are less likely to recall their feelings about intangible characteristics of products and services when they aren't in the process of using them	using the actual products or prototype, or engaging in the actual activity for which an innovation is being designed, stimulates comments about such intangibles as smells or emotions associated with the product's use

Inquiry	Observation
people's imagination – and hence their desires – are bounded by their experience, they accept inadequacies and deficiencies in their environment as normal	trained, technically sophisticated observers can see solutions to unarticulated needs
questions are often biased and reflect enquirers' unrecognized assumptions	observation is open-ended and varied; trained observers tend to cancel out one another's observational biases
questioning interrupts the usual flow of people's natural activity	observation, while almost never totally unobtrusive, interrupts normal activities less than questioning does
questioning stifles opportunities for users to suggest innovations	observers in the field often identify user innovations that can be duplicated and improved for the rest of the market

Source: Leonard and Rayport, 1997

(Source of article: von Stamm, 2003, pp. 117–124)

Discussion

Von Stamm is critical of both quantitative and qualitative approaches to market research as ways of finding out the information that is needed when developing radically new products. In the next section I will be addressing the question that she poses: 'Given that traditional approaches do not work too well, particularly in the context of innovation, what then are the approaches that might help?' The focus in the next section will be on how designers and innovators can create products that will be successful in the marketplace.

Key points of Section 3

- Understanding markets so that decisions can be made about new and existing products requires the gathering of information from a wide range of sources. The system for collecting together this information is known as the marketing decision support system.

- The marketing decision support system has the task of supplying several different types of information at all stages of product development and sales.

- Information about markets is used for strategic planning for the future, new product development and sales and marketing strategies.

- There are two kinds of sources of information for market research. Primary sources are where potential purchasers are directly involved in the research. Secondary sources are where published reports cover a general market area.

- An understanding of the market environment requires an understanding of societal trends, lifestyle changes, trends, legislation and scientific advances.

- Market research is one of the key ways of gathering information from primary sources.

- Market research can be either quantitative or qualitative. However all research has to be valid and all should go through the same five steps: define, plan, research, analyse, report.

- Research can be carried out using personal means such as individual or group interviews, or impersonal means such as postal and internet surveys and point-of-sale information gathering.

- Finding out information for the development of innovations and radically new products may require techniques other than those commonly used for market research.

4 Markets and design

4.1 Using market information in design

Market research on its own might be well conceived and come up with the most interesting insights and revelations, but its true value will depend upon the communication between those who carry out the research and those in other sections of the company who have to apply their findings and recommendations.

To launch a successful innovation it is crucial that there is good communication between all those involved in the product development process, from those designing the products through to those concerned with gathering information on the market.

The reality in many companies in the past was that the liaison between marketing and the research, design and development departments was poor. The marketing department was only called in to sell the product after it had been designed, or was called in for an opinion at a late stage of the product development. Now, however, many companies have adopted a more integrated approach.

Later in this block, you will learn more about how designers themselves are considering users and their experiences. In this section, however, I will look at the ways market research informs designers during decision-making.

4.2 Marketing mix and the four Ps

In order to brief designers, decision-makers within companies have to make judgements about a number of factors that will affect both the design and the success of a product. These factors are known as the *marketing mix*.

The marketing mix used to be known as the *4 Ps*, because the four factors that were originally identified all began with the letter P. Over time other factors have been identified that also affect the marketing mix and the success of a product. And in keeping with the past, the new factors use words beginning with P.

The new factors have been added by various authors on marketing and reflect the increasing sophistication of goods and services and the need to consider other factors such as aftersales service and features that add to the attractiveness of the product.

Exercise 10 Factors in the mix

Before I tell you, what do you think the factors that affect the success of a product might be? Remember the factors need to begin with the letter P.

Discussion

What did you put? Read the rest of this section to find out about the Ps of the marketing mix.

The factors in the marketing mix are as follows.

Original 4 Ps

- product
- price
- place
- promotion.

Added factors

- process
- physical evidence
- properties
- pleasure
- people.

Some of these factors of the marketing mix influence the success of the product or innovation but are outside the scope of the product designer. In the explanation that follows, I will look at these factors in terms of how they influence product design.

4.3 Product

This aspect of the marketing mix is the one upon which designers have the most direct impact. If a company is to succeed in the marketplace, it needs to have a product that will attract buyers. When people buy products, they weigh up the attributes of the products they see to choose between similar products. Some of the attributes that purchasers consider are given in Table 5.

Table 5 Attributes considered by purchasers

Attribute	Considerations
Function	What does the product do? What are its features?
Performance	How well does the product do what it claims? How much will it cost to run?
Ease of use	How easy is it to use? How complex is it to understand?
Reliability	How robust and reliable is it?
Aesthetics	Is it pleasing to look at?
Image	What image does it convey?
Compatibility	Does it work with other products? Is it compatible with the purchaser's values?

Each attribute in Table 5 will need to be designed into the product.

During the development stages of a product the designers will use market research intelligence together with their own experience and knowledge to shape these attributes.

4.3.1 Product differentiation

As I have discussed previously products are designed with particular segments of the potential marketplace in mind, and companies offer a range of products for different pockets, preferences and needs. Creating different versions of the same basic product is known as *product differentiation*.

Product differentiation is important to companies for two reasons, firstly to ensure that products sell to as many different markets as possible, and secondly because differentiation is what distinguishes one company's products from those of its competitors. Individual products convey to the potential purchaser messages about quality, style and image and affect how potential purchasers perceive the company and its product range as a whole.

Many companies strive to create *brand loyalty* in their customers and achieve this partly through the qualities of products themselves and partly through advertising and packaging that creates a certain image of the company.

4.3.2 Brands

A strong brand name is of immense value to a company. Branding is about the reputation of the company's products and their perceived value. Most large companies spend time and money on finding ways to promote their brand and to create positive associations with the brand name in the minds of potential purchasers. Promotion may be through advertising campaigns, company conferences or roadshows – an example of the latter is the annual Apple Expo, at which new Apple computers are launched.

Trademarks and registered designs may be strongly associated with a brand. In some cases, customers can identify products from particular manufacturers at a glance – for example the badges on cars enable you to distinguish the manufacturer easily (Figure 26). Colours, shapes, typography and even interfaces can become recognised as belonging to a particular brand. Think about the trademarks of the Coca Cola Company, the red and white colours used on the packaging, the shape of the original Coca Cola bottle and the lettering that is immediately recognisable, even by people who cannot read.

Most large companies routinely look for infringements of trademarks and copies of their designs, and take legal action to defend their rights. One of the things that companies look out for is the use of their brand name as a general term. For example the company name Hoover has become synonymous with vacuum cleaner. Use of brand names in this way can desensitise the potential purchaser to the merits of the particular brand, so companies will often take action if such indiscriminate use of their brand name is seen in the media.

Although all of the attributes of the product affect the purchasing decision there are some factors that are fundamental for a product to stand any chance of success. These factors are performance and reliability. If a product is flawed technically or fails because it breaks down after a short time, it is unlikely to last long in the market. Sales may be buoyant at first, but once word gets around that a product is

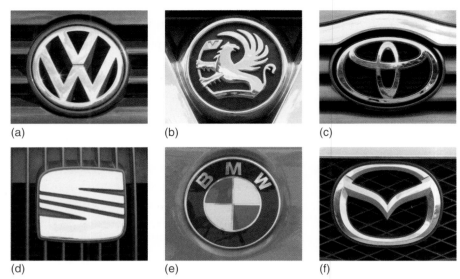

Figure 26   Car badges enable the manufacturer to be recognised at a glance

unreliable, sales will probably decline rapidly, possibly harming the reputation of the brand as a whole. In such a situation the manufacturers may have to invest a lot of money to correct the technical problems and overcome the negative publicity.

Another factor that is particularly crucial to an innovative product is whether that product offers a relative advantage over existing solutions.

Designers therefore have a responsibility to create products that work and last as long as is reasonable for the product type. If these factors are addressed, the other factors, such as the features, look and feel of the product, will become important determinants of success.

Exercise 11   What's your brand?

Write down a list of the brands or companies that you are loyal to, if any. What is it about these companies' products that appeals to you? Are there any brands of products that you would not consider buying? Why is this?

Discussion

Perhaps my strongest loyalty is to Apple Macintosh computers. I used one to write this block at work and I have two at home. I think Apple products are reliable, robust, easy to use and well styled. I do not have any conscious dislikes of brands but, having said that, I probably would not consider buying a product that did not fit my self-image. I would also think twice about buying a product that had not fared well in tests carried out by the Consumers' Association magazine *Which*, but I would only look for this information for high-value products such as white goods and cameras. Although I would not consider myself a 'dark green' environmentalist, I do consider the social and environmental impact of products I buy, which sometimes influences my purchasing decisions.

4.3.3 Product standardisation

Standards have become increasingly important as products become more technically complex and costly to develop. The term standards is used in relation to products in several ways and it is important to distinguish between them.

Government standards

Firstly there are standards that are set by government, which set out certain technical expectations with which a product must comply. Government standards are set largely to ensure safety and quality in products and are concerned with general aspects such as electrical safety. They are not intended to favour one product above another, although manufacturers often advise governments on the setting of standards and do have a vested interest in the outcome.

In some industries in the past, government standards have acted as a trade barrier to limit imports. For example German standards for electrical products such as lighting were at one time more rigorous than UK standards and effectively limited UK trade in that country to those companies who were able and willing to change their products to meet these higher standards. In the same way Japan has used standards to restrict the import of foreign cars. Designers have to meet the government standards for any country in which it is proposed to sell the product.

Standardisation of components

Standardisation is also used to describe the use of standard shapes and sizes of components, to enable parts to be interchangeable. Designers need to be aware of components that are already in use in other company products, and components that are available 'off the shelf'. Alternatively they may design new components that can be used in a range of products to help keep manufacturing costs down.

Industry standards

Although government standards and standardisation undoubtedly affect the form and nature of the product, industry standards perhaps have the most direct impact on the purchaser and end user. Industry standards are specifications agreed by manufacturers in the industry to ensure a degree of compatibility between products. These standards concern whole products, and from the user's point of view they enable products from different manufacturers to be interchanged.

Most people will have some experience of the issues that surround this form of standardisation. The last few decades of the twentieth century were a time of rapid technological development. In this climate many new products emerged, some of which performed the identical function but achieved this in different ways.

A classic example is the development of video tape for the domestic market. Two different products were developed in parallel. Sony developed the Betamax video system while JVC developed the VHS system. Although both systems made acceptable video recordings, the cassettes from one system could not be used in the other. It is generally accepted that Betamax was technically superior, and a development of this system is still used for professional recordings. However, when first launched, JVC had a longer recording time of

2 hours, whereas Betamax could only record for 1 hour. JVC machines were therefore able to record feature films, whereas Betamax recorders were not.

However it was company strategy rather than product qualities that decided VHS would be the dominant format. JVC took the shrewd decision to allow other companies to produce VHS recorders and cassettes under licence. This strategy meant that VHS quickly dominated the market and set the standard for future video cassette recorder developments.

Similar issues surrounded the introduction of the first DVDs, which succeeded the video cassette. Several companies worked on this technology in parallel, and a number of formats appeared on the market that were incompatible with each other. Eventually a dominant format emerged for prerecorded films, and manufacturers of DVD players created machines that are capable of detecting and playing a number of different DVD formats. However for home DVD recording the format issue remained a problem for some time.

There is a similar story for formats for downloading music from the internet. Here, various companies developed different formats to try to dominate the market. In this case the formats were linked to the development of music players, some of which were deliberately only compatible with one format.

The nature of the product undoubtedly has some effect on whether a non-standard product can compete in a competitive field. If the product is self-contained, the only problems that might arise concern the availability of spare parts, and if the manufacturer is prepared to supply these, this is not a difficulty.

However if the product requires inputs such as CDs, DVDs or computer software, this changes the situation. Such products are concerned with information in various forms, most of which is produced by a different set of companies.

Where there is a need for new inputs and updating of information, the move to set standards is the strongest. The battle is won either by the company that can produce enough of its own software to make the product attractive or by the company that can persuade information and software providers to create products for its hardware.

Collaboration and standards

Some companies are now taking a new approach to product development, driven in part by the desire to set industry standards. Companies are collaborating to develop products, particularly for the mid- to long-term future. This is seen particularly in the development of consumer electronics. Royal Philips Electronics, one of the global leaders in electronics for all sectors, has collaborated with clothing manufacturers Levi and Nike to develop wearable electronics and with manufacturers such as Sony to develop new home entertainment systems (Figure 27).

Figure 27   Products such as the DesXcape detachable monitor made by Philips have come about as a result of collaborative research on connected homes as explored in the Unihome project Source: Philips Electronics UK Ltd

Exercise 12   Sticking to standards

Can you think of any other examples where the success of a new product depends upon industry standards and products developed by other manufacturers?

Discussion

There are lots of examples where the success of a new product is dependent upon products developed by other manufacturers, particularly within the field of communication and information technologies. Any product requiring an information input, such as a CD or DVD drive, information from the internet or information from other machines, will need to be compatible with the products and information with which it has to interface. All computer accessories such as printers, external drives, USB flash cards and digital cameras have to be able to communicate with the computer to which they are attached.

> ### Box 4 Cautionary tale
>
> It may seem that a company that wins the standardisation battle has won the marketing war, but this is not necessarily the case. The IBM personal computer became the industry standard in the 1980s. IBM, whose main business was in large, mainframe computers, approached the task of building a microcomputer using components that were freely available from other manufacturers. This open-source approach meant that other companies wishing to enter the personal computer market could take IBM's model and produce their own compatible version.
>
> The problem for IBM was that these companies then became competitors, producing their own versions of the personal computer more cheaply. By the 1990s, IBM was in serious financial trouble because, as the market for computers became increasingly competitive, IBM did not have a big enough share of the market to save it from difficulty.
>
> Interestingly the companies who have made the biggest profits from the diffusion of personal computers are not the companies assembling the whole machines, but the chip manufacturers, Intel and AMD, whose chips are at the heart of non-Apple personal computers. Manufacturing the components on which designs are standardised can be a lucrative business.

4.3.4 Trigger and incremental products

Another aspect of product development affecting the design process is the distinction between trigger and incremental products. *Trigger products* are the key products in a company's product range that will prompt a potential customer to make a purchase. *Incremental products* are ones that on their own would not be enough to prompt a purchase but are add-ons to the main products.

In computing, the trigger products are the computer hardware and main software packages, whereas the incremental products are software utilities such as the desk accessories, screen savers and games.

Trigger and incremental products are also found in service industries. For example the trigger product of a bank may be its financial services but a range of incremental services, such as insurance policies for travel, home and life, can also be offered to customers.

The marketing strategies for trigger and incremental products will be different. A trigger product will be sold on its intrinsic merit, whereas an incremental product will be sold on the good will created by the trigger product as much as on its own worth. The designer therefore has to achieve consistent quality between trigger and incremental products to maintain the reputation of the brand.

Mobile telephones provide another example of trigger and incremental products. The main purchase is the phone itself, but most models have additional options and services that can be bought to enhance what it offers. The quality of these accessories and enhancements may well determine which brand of phone is purchased in the first place.

4.4 Price

The next element of the marketing mix, and one of the constraints within which a designer has to work when designing a new product, is that of price. The designer has to achieve a compromise between the requirements of the manufacturer, which will almost invariably be to keep manufacturing costs as low as possible, and the requirements of the user to have value for money.

Pricing is a complex business, and it can be crucial to the success or failure of a product. If the price is too high, there may not be a large enough market, because there may not be enough potential purchasers who can afford it. Conversely if the price is too low, people may be put off from buying a good product because they will perceive it as too cheap to have value. Although the pricing strategy for a product is not usually determined by the designer, this strategy will significantly affect the design of the product and the messages it communicates.

4.4.1 Determining price

The pricing strategies that companies adopt depend upon the objectives the companies have set themselves. For example one company may be seeking to maintain or expand its share of a certain market, another to reach a certain level of return on investment, and yet another to achieve a steady rate of growth or to keep up a planned level of output from its production facilities.

Market research is used to evaluate the level of potential sales that might be expected within different price bands. Research is also needed to establish the elasticity of the demand. *Elasticity of demand* is the measure of how much demand would change with a small change in price. If the demand for the product remains the same when there is a price change, it is said to be inelastic but if it changes greatly, it is said to be elastic. For the designer the goal is to create a product that has sufficient appeal to be bought by purchasers even if the price fluctuates a little.

Gauging the demand, and hence the price, for radically new products is harder than for products that are improvements on existing ones. In many cases the market research for radically new products is conducted to establish what the market will bear – in other words the highest price that can be charged to reach an economically viable level of sales.

The decision-makers in a manufacturing company that is producing products to be sold through a distribution chain have to consider the price the final purchaser might be willing to pay, and work backwards from there to establish the price they will ask from the wholesaler. Companies selling directly to the final purchaser do not have to concern themselves with ensuring that sufficient profit is made by each link of the distribution chain. However such companies are likely to be submitting tenders or quotes to the purchaser for them to choose between manufacturers. In such a situation it is important to get the pricing right – to be competitive but also to make a profit.

The other side of the pricing equation is to work out the costs of production and distribution for different levels of sales. Costs will vary in accordance with the number of items produced. Some costs are fixed, for example the cost of the production facility and tooling, and other costs are variable, for example the costs of raw materials. A high volume of sales will generally mean a lower cost per unit than a low volume of sales, and this may be taken into account in establishing the optimum price for the product.

Demand for a product will generally establish the maximum price that can be charged, and the costs of production will determine the minimum price that is acceptable. The price will be set within this band between the maximum and minimum prices depending on how the company wishes the product to be viewed. Most companies will look at the prices of competing products. If the product is radically new and breaking new ground, this analysis may have to be performed by looking at comparable rather than identical products.

Setting the final price will depend upon the pricing method that has been selected.

Cost-plus pricing

Cost-plus pricing is a common method that involves estimating the average cost of producing and marketing a product item and adding a mark-up for profit. Many small traders will use this method, for example your local baker or craftsperson.

Demand pricing

Demand pricing is a more sophisticated method in which account is taken of the variation in costs of production at different levels of sales. Charts are produced to show the break-even point at various levels of sales. The costs of production at each level are weighed against the possible level of sales, and the price chosen is that which will yield the greatest profit. Manufacturing companies and super-retailers who have commissioned own brand products may use this method to determine the price of a product. For example a company may look at whether the cost of installing new production facilities to increase the number of units that can be made and reduce the cost per item would produce a greater profit than using existing equipment and producing fewer items at a higher price (Figure 28).

Competitor-based pricing

A company may choose not to use either costs or demand as its guide, but to set its price in relation to its competitors. This could mean setting prices to the same level or setting them slightly lower to under-cut them. A company with a large market share may be in the position of being the price leader for the industry and may be able to adjust prices without losing significant sales.

Product-line pricing

Product-line pricing is when prices are set for linked product groups. An example of this is computer printers. The prices of printers are kept deliberately low to encourage purchase but the manufacturers make their profits on repeated purchases of ink cartridges and specialist paper.

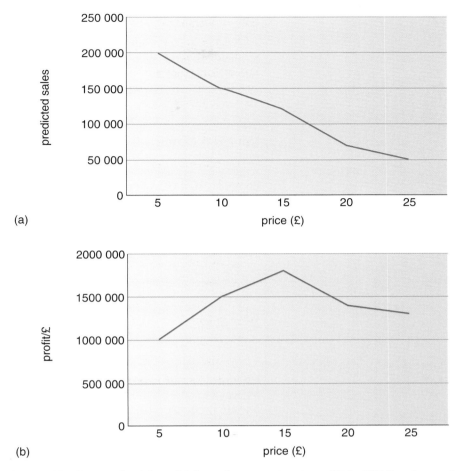

(a)

(b)

Figure 28 Demand pricing: (a) for prices ranging from £5 to £25 the demand can be predicted; (b) using the figures for predicted demand the price can be established that will give the best profit

Psychological pricing

There are a number of psychological pricing methods, for example setting the price in accordance with the perceived value of the product. *Prestige pricing* is a method used to appeal to the most affluent end of the market. Alternatively prices can be set at *significant price bands*, for example €9.99 or £9.99.

An awareness of the pricing strategy used is important for designers and innovators from an early stage of product development. Different pricing strategies will cause designers to focus on different aspects of the product.

Exercise 13   How price affects design

How do you think each of the pricing strategies described above might affect the design of products?

Discussion

Cost-plus pricing

The emphasis for product development will be on designing to achieve low manufacturing costs.

Demand pricing

Depending on where the price level has been set, the designer will be seeking to minimise production costs while maximising customer appeal to achieve the target level of sales.

Competitor-based pricing

The designer will need to evaluate competitors' products to develop a product that has comparable features. If the aim is to take a larger share of the market, the designer may look at ways of adding value to the product and making it more attractive than the competition. If the aim is to undercut the competition, the designer will be looking at ways to reduce production costs without noticeably compromising the product.

Product-line pricing

The designer will have to aim to give good value for money and reliability on the trigger product while keeping production costs low. To encourage repeat purchases, the incremental accessories will need to be attractive and easy to use. The accessories may also be made specifically to fit the product so that the purchaser has to purchase the accessories made by that manufacturer.

Psychological pricing

For prestige pricing and to create perceived value, the designer will be looking for ways to convey the feeling of a quality product. For significant price band pricing, production costs may need to be kept as low as possible to achieve the target price.

4.5 Place

In the marketing mix the term place is used in its broadest sense to describe how a product gets from the manufacturer to the final purchaser. Manufacturers need to ensure the product reaches the target market by getting it to the right place at the right time.

The distribution of the product may be *geographical*, for example a particular area of the country, or may involve types of *physical places* such as retail outlets or wholesalers. In some sectors however there may be sales direct from the manufacturer to the purchaser.

Considerations of where a product is to be sold may affect the design in several ways, in terms of how it looks, how it works, what it does, the materials it uses and its properties. Increasingly designers are also concerned about distribution issues, particularly minimising costs through weight reduction and creating packaging that allows as many as possible to be packed into a container. Although often driven by a desire to lower costs, this approach to design has an important benefit of improving the environmental impact of products by a reduction in the use of resources and a reduction in the use of fuel to distribute the product.

4.5.1 Geographical placing

Companies also have to decide on the geographical markets in which to sell their products. Market preferences vary internationally and regionally. A product that sells well in Glasgow may not necessarily find such a good market in Brighton.

You have already seen that standards and regulations can be a barrier to some international trade but there are also different cultural preferences in different countries, which have to be taken into account if a company wants to sell its products abroad. Markets have now become globalised, with many large companies now selling the same basic product all over the world, sometimes using the same promotional campaigns. In these multinational companies it is the design team's job to create a product with universal appeal, although this is not always possible.

Philips Design looked at the markets for vacuum cleaners. It wanted to produce one design that could be sold in both European and Asian markets. However its research with users showed the cultural differences were great – each continent had different preferences for the attributes of the product, such as colour and shape. This meant that a compromise was not possible, so it was considered less risky to design two different cleaners, to meet the needs of each market.

4.5.2 Physical placing

Ensuring that a product reaches the customer at the appropriate time is essential for the successful diffusion of innovations. Although this depends mostly upon the production and distribution systems within the manufacturing company, the designer has a role in ensuring the product design is straightforward to manufacture and that it can be packed efficiently for distribution.

Another implication for the designer is in the choice of components. Innovations sometimes fail to reach the market on time because a bought-in component has been found to be faulty or unreliable. Specifying and sourcing reliable components is crucial to enable production to proceed to schedule.

4.6 Promotion

If a company's products are to succeed, the public must know about these products. The fourth element in the marketing mix is promotion. For designers in a large company the involvement in promotion may be limited to a team of packaging designers. In a smaller company designers may be involved in the creation of both packaging and promotional materials.

Promotion is about image creation, both for the company and for specific products, and about creating loyalty to brands and products in various ways, including the use of monetary incentives. The main forms of promotion are *sales promotion*, *advertising*, *publicity* and *personal selling*, all of which are used in different combinations in different circumstances.

Exercise 14   Image or product?

A lot of the advertising that takes place is concerned with the creation of a company or brand image rather than the sale of a specific product. Watch an advertisement break on television, look at the advertising in a magazine or newspaper and look at any hoardings near to where you live. How many of these advertisements are concerned with specific products and how many with company or brand image?

Discussion

On the television, you probably found that specific consumable products such as toiletries and food products are advertised individually, as are certain models of car. This is because the cost of television advertising is so great it is used mostly for high-value products such as cars or repeat-purchase products such as foods and toiletries. There are exceptions to this, particularly if a new product, such as a computer, is being launched. There are also times, such as during children's programmes, when individual toys and games are promoted.

Newspaper and magazine advertising is mixed – large colour advertisements frequently support television advertising campaigns but may also contain advertisements for individual products. Hoardings often contain advertisements about company image rather than specific products.

In the commercial and public market sectors there may be some advertising in relevant journals. Often though, purchasing decisions are made either through contact with company representatives or based on photographs in a catalogue or on the internet. In the latter situations the product has to communicate its desirability in a two-dimensional image. So designers need to design products that communicate to purchasers through their visual appearance.

If the qualities of a product are not being promoted directly through advertising, the product on the shelf must communicate with potential purchasers through its appearance, qualities and functions.

4.7   New P factors

The factors that have been identified more recently as being important to the marketing mix are concerned less directly with the development of the product and are more to do with the way it is bought and sold. These factors are important determinants of how a new product is taken up and diffused in the market. The new Ps described below are process, physical evidence, properties, pleasure and people.

4.7.1 Process

The process of purchasing a product may affect how readily it is adopted by the market. If the process is too complicated, potential purchasers may be reluctant to make the effort to buy it. Successful diffusion onto the market is affected by the product's availability, delivery and aftersales service.

A difficult acquisition process or problems with maintenance may put off prospective purchasers, although there are some high-value exceptions. For example there are waiting lists of months or even years for some bespoke cars.

The most complex purchasing decisions are often those where products and services are interdependent, such as information technology products. The purchasing process can be complicated by several factors:

- services and related products sold separately, for example computers requiring internet service providers to enable access to the internet

- overwhelming amount of choice, for example many different service providers and many different models of mobile phone

- need for explanation of the product for the potential purchaser to understand its potential benefits.

Case study   Freeview

In the UK, in 2002, a number of free-to-view digital television channels were launched in anticipation of the eventual move away from analogue to digital broadcasting. To view these channels means having a satellite receiver, a compatible cable system or a Freeview box (Figure 29). A BBC advertising campaign promoting the new channels offered a helpline number through which interested parties could find out more about how to use the hardware needed to access these channels.

Figure 29   Freeview box that delivers digital TV channels and an interactive service Source: Tom Porter

The BBC is relying on the diffusion of Freeview boxes to fulfil government targets of a complete changeover to digital television in the UK by 2010.

In order to buy the required hardware the potential purchaser needs to consider:

- whether their home can receive the digital signal, whether it is within transmitter range and whether they have a digital aerial – in summer 2004 only 75 per cent of households in the UK could receive the digital signal

- which local retailers stock the set-top boxes, and which box to buy

- whether they feel confident enough to install the box themselves.

However the complexity of this purchasing process is counterbalanced by the fact that a one-off purchase is all that is needed and there is no contract or ongoing cost.

In June 2003, research showed that, of those subscribing to the new service, 45 per cent were over the age of 55 – significantly more than for cable or digital satellite services, both of which have around 26 per cent of the over-55s. The simplicity of a one-off purchase with no contract was identified as the single most important feature for 65 per cent of those who had purchased a Freeview box.

A report by Ofcom in 2004 estimated that by the end of December 2003, more than 50 per cent (over 12 million) of all UK households had digital television. Of the 3.2 million households receiving free-to-air digital television channels, nearly 3 million were receiving these through a Freeview box.

4.7.2 Physical evidence

When a purchase of a product is made the purchaser has the physical evidence of the product itself. However when purchasing a service, there may be little or no physical evidence to reassure the purchaser. In service industries such as banking, confirmation that the purchaser has made the right decision may be reinforced by brochures or even free gifts. For someone buying a digital service such as access to information or digital products, there needs to be evidence to show that the service is available. For example an icon might appear on screen when the service is not in use and a branded interface will appear when the service is selected (Figure 30).

Figure 30　Yell.com allows the user to access its database on a mobile phone. The interface uses colours that convey the brand identity of this directory provider. Source VisMedia

4.7.3 Properties

The properties factor is strongly related to the product factor in the original 4 Ps. However the product embraces a wide range of attributes, of which properties are only a small part. It is useful therefore to consider the aesthetic and environmental properties of a product as strong elements of the marketing mix in their own right. Aesthetics, or how the product looks, is of obvious importance with all fashion products, including furniture and furnishings. However many other products, particularly consumer electronics, will be purchased for their aesthetic qualities as much as how well they perform.

For other purchasers the environmental properties of a product may be important. This is seen most strongly in food, where, in the UK, as in other northern European countries, organic food is sought out by a sizable percentage of the population. Purchasers of white goods also may consider the energy rating of a product when comparing similar products, although their motives may be partly environmental and partly financial. The number of consumers actively seeking out eco-products is relatively small but many purchasers are influenced to some degree by manufacturers' claims that products are environmentally friendly, non-toxic or recyclable.

4.7.4 People

Although this factor was identified first in relation to service industries, people can be important to the diffusion of product innovations. With a radically new product it is important that the people selling it understand how the product works and what its benefits are, so that this can be communicated to would-be purchasers. People also provide any aftersales service and support, and the service they offer may affect perceptions of the product that will influence future purchasing decisions. Some manufacturers offer training or hold events to inform sales people about the benefits of their radically new product.

An example of what happens when the people talking directly to purchasers do not understand the product is the introduction of condensing boilers onto the marketplace. Condensing boilers offer significant opportunities for saving energy in the home. However when they were first introduced the uptake of these boilers was slow in the UK because many plumbers, who were asked for advice by potential purchasers, did not understand the technology and found reasons not to recommend them.

4.7.5 Pleasure

The pleasure that a purchaser derives from a product is known as *added value*. A product may work really well and do everything it says on the box, but if it also gives the user a lot of pleasure to use, it has an advantage over the competition. Most classic designs that have endured for years have this value-added factor. Designing a product that delights purchasers can lead to levels of sales being sustained for a longer period. The Apple iPod attained almost iconic status, partly because of its aesthetic and partly because of the pleasure derived from the use of the product (Figure 31).

Figure 31 Apple iPod personal music player

In Section 6 you will see how designers have taken this need to add value and to delight users to the core of their practice. Increasingly delight and pleasure are being used to differentiate products and services and win markets, and this is now an important aspect of the marketing mix.

SAQ 14

What are the original 4 Ps of the marketing mix? Briefly explain their significance for designers.

SAQ 15

What are the new Ps of the marketing mix? Briefly explain their significance for designers.

SAQ 16

Identify three ways standards affect the design of products.

Exercise 15   Where does sustainability fit?

Where do you think sustainability fits into the marketing mix?

Discussion

In marketing literature, sustainability is not discussed as a separate element of the marketing mix. However companies that have a sustainability policy might incorporate sustainability criteria into their brief for some elements of the marketing mix. For example a company may achieve this by incorporating it into any of the elements of product, place, promotion, properties or people.

- For the element of *product* a company may actively seek to reduce the environmental impact by such measures as making use of fewer or more environmentally friendly materials or reducing the energy use of the product.

- For the element of *place* the company may reduce the use of materials leading to reduced transportation costs, or even set up local production of product using locally available materials and labour.

- For the element of *promotion* the environmental and wider sustainability benefits may be communicated through promotional materials or packaging design.

- For the element of *properties* the design of the product may communicate a positive message about its environmental benefits or wider sustainability issues such as fair trade.

- For the element of *people* those individuals selling the product may be trained or educated about the benefits and best way to use the product to reduce energy use or other environmental impacts.

I hope that as people become more aware of the need to consider issues of sustainability, another P might be added to the marketing mix, namely P for planet.

4.8   Product life cycle

The term life cycle is used in several ways when discussing products. Firstly it is used to discuss how long an individual product will last until it wears out and needs replacement. Secondly it is used to discuss the environmental impact of a product at different stages of its life, manufacture, use and disposal. However the term life cycle is also used to describe the different stages that a particular product design goes through from its initial launch through to its eventual obsolescence (Figure 32).

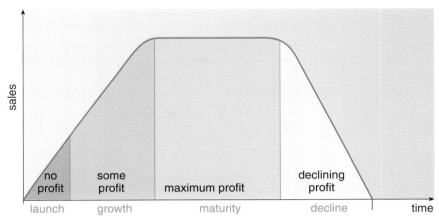

Figure 32 **Product life cycle showing the rise and fall of sales at different stages** Source: Open University, 1996

However well a product is designed, it will not last indefinitely. You will be used to seeing products come onto the market, sell for a while and eventually disappear. The length of time that a product remains on the market will depend upon a number of factors:

- nature of the product – what the product is
- technical complexity – how complicated the product is technically
- production processes – how the product is manufactured
- sales – how well it is selling
- demands of the market – whether the market is demanding changes.

Many technologically simple products, such as ballpoint pens and basic razors, which achieve high volume of sales, have lengthy life cycles. Frequently these life cycles are longer than those of complex products, such as computers, for which technology is rapidly developing. However it is often the case with complex products that many of the basic components remain the same for several generations of product, even though other features are improved incrementally to create 'new' generations of product.

There are several stages in the life of a product. These stages are discussed below.

4.8.1 Stage 1 – Introduction and launch

Firstly there is the phase of introduction or product launch. This period is often characterised by a slow growth of sales as the product starts to be taken up by the market. During this period the company incurs many costs associated with the launch and so there is little or no profit.

4.8.2 Stage 2 – Growth

After the initial launch period there follows a time when the market gradually accepts the product and it begins to diffuse. In this period profits rise substantially and there is a steady growth in sales.

4.8.3 Stage 3 – Maturity

Maturity is reached when sales reach a steady level. In this period profits per unit remain stable, or decline slightly if the company has to spend money to sell the product in a competitive marketplace.

4.8.4 Stage 4 – Decline

The period of decline begins when market saturation has been reached. Sales begin to drop off and do not revive, and profits fall. At this point the company has to decide what level of profit is acceptable and whether to continue making the product.

In Section 1 you saw the stages of the product life cycle mapped onto the market innovation spiral (Figure 8). This spiral shows the cyclical nature of product design. When a product design reaches the end of its life, the process of product development begins again. However the spiral nature of this model shows the starting point for the new generation of product design is further forward than the starting point for the original design.

Some companies make deliberate decisions to keep the lives of their product designs short and to produce new, improved products at frequent intervals, rather than waiting for the maturity and decline stages of the product life cycle. The aim of this strategy is to stimulate sales by convincing purchasers to have the latest version of a product. It is also a strategy to maintain a market advantage over slower competitors. This strategy is known as *product churning* and it can be seen most clearly in the consumer electronics and fashion industries.

The graphs in Figure 33 show that different life-cycle curves can be drawn for different sorts of products. The graphs show sales of products over a fixed period. Some products will have a relatively short life, appearing perhaps for a season and then disappearing. Some children's playthings fall into this category (Figure 34). Others will have a steady volume of sales for many years – classic designs such as the Anglepoise desk light (Figure 35) fall into this category, alongside more mundane objects such as light bulbs and stationery items. Some products take a long time to diffuse into the market but then sell well for some time, before gradually declining in popularity. Others go into a rapid decline when a new technological solution or better-designed product comes along.

When a novel product is first launched, the market's expectations of it are limited but as purchasers become more familiar with the innovation their expectations of it will become more sophisticated. Some people are keen to buy a product when it has just been launched and others like to wait to see whether the product is reliable or worthwhile before making the decision to purchase it. Those people who buy a newly launched product may seek the status associated with a state-of-the-art innovation but they are also taking a risk.

The first generation of a radically new product may quickly be bettered by successive generations as technological teething problems are sorted out. In the early life of a product, purchasers may be prepared to put up with minor problems that later on in the product's life would be unacceptable.

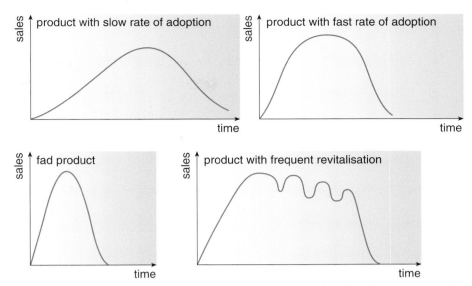

Figure 33   **Sales of products with different rates of adoption** Source: adapted from Assael, 1990

Figure 34   **The Tamagotchi is an example of a fad children's toy, which is relaunched periodically in a slightly modified form**

Purchasers can be classified into five categories of buying behaviour:

- Innovators

  Innovators are the people who are first to buy new products. They are prepared to risk possible problems for the benefit of being one of the first people to own that product.

- Early adopters

  Early adopters wait a little to see how innovators fare with new products but follow them by purchasing a product early on in its life cycle.

- Early majority

  Early majority purchasers wait to see that a product has become established before deciding to buy.

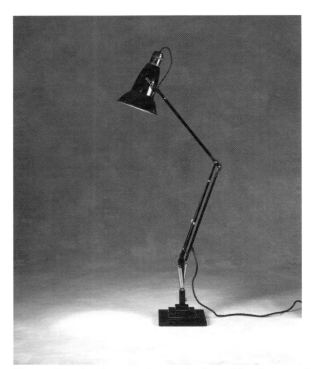

Figure 35   Anglepoise lamp, designed by George Carwardine in 1932. This product remained virtually unchanged for 50 years and was the manufacturer's only product for much of this time. Source: Science and Society Picture Library

- Late majority

  The late majority hold back on purchasing new products but do buy them when they are well-diffused onto the marketplace.

- Forced adopters (laggards)

  Forced adopters (sometimes called laggards) purchase new products late in the product life cycle, either because they no longer have a choice or because the price has come down sufficiently to enable them to make purchases.

SAQ 17

Draw a diagram of the product life cycle and show where the five categories of purchasers described above make their purchases.

4.8.5   Price and the product life cycle

At different points of a product's life cycle the price of that product may vary. The strategy adopted for pricing a product will change as the product matures and will be heavily influenced by manufacturing costs and demand for the product. Early in a product's life, when costs are relatively high, it may be offered at a high price. Later in the life cycle, when costs have been reduced by improvements in the production process or the economies of large-scale production, the price may fall.

Introductory phase

In the introductory phase of a product's life, various pricing strategies are possible and their relationship is shown in Figure 36.

	Promotion high	Promotion low
High price	rapid skimming	slow skimming
Low price	rapid penetration	slow penetration

Figure 36 Pricing and promotional strategies Source: adapted from Open University, 1996

Market penetration is achieved by pricing the product low to stimulate sales. In contrast *market skimming* is where the product is priced high to reach a smaller target market and create an image of exclusiveness and quality.

Both of these strategies can be employed with either a low or a high level of promotion. If high levels of promotion are used, these strategies are referred to as rapid penetration or rapid skimming. If low levels of promotion are used, these strategies are referred to as slow penetration or slow skimming. The amount of promotional activity chosen will depend upon the competing products and the understanding and reaction of potential purchasers.

Growth stage

In the growth stage of a product's life the aim of the manufacturer will be to keep prices steady in order to encourage new and repeat purchases. However in this phase of a product's life, once the competition is known, it is possible that either the price of the product can be reduced to make the product more competitive or that new features can be added to the basic product to offer added value for the same price.

Maturity stage

In the maturity stage of the life cycle, strategies of price reduction or added value might be adopted to try to stimulate market demand, and special price offers might be used to reawaken interest in the product.

Decline stage

In the decline phase of a product's life, decisions have to be made about how long the declining product can be sustained. The strategies adopted may not involve price changes but the company will look for ways to cut the costs it incurs in producing, distributing and marketing the product. For some products the decline phase will be short because there will be new products waiting to take that product's place, but for other products this decline phase may be lengthy. Manufacturers are often reluctant to abandon a product that has a loyal following until the financial implications of continuing with it are untenable.

SAQ 18

What pricing strategies might be adopted at different stages of the product life cycle?

Key points of Section 4

- There are a number of factors that need to be communicated to designers to inform the design process. These factors are known as the marketing mix.

- Originally there were 4 Ps identified as important factors in the marketing mix – these are product, price, place and promotion. However other related factors have now been added: process, physical evidence, properties, pleasure and people.

- The product aspect of the marketing mix is the aspect that designers have most direct impact on. Designers often create different versions of the same basic product to meet different market needs.

- Standards and standardisation can be important determinants of market success, as well as being constraints on the product design.

- It is useful to consider whether a product is a key trigger product or an incremental enhancement to an existing product.

- Pricing a product is complex and takes into account different factors, such as production costs, the volume of demand and psychological factors. There are a number of pricing methods adopted by companies, all of which affect the design of products in various ways: cost-plus pricing, demand pricing, competitor-based pricing, product-line pricing and psychological pricing.

- The places where a product is to be sold will affect the design of products. Effects may be aesthetic and functional, meeting different cultural preferences and desires. Matters of weight, materials and distribution are also considered.

- Promotion of products is often done through advertising but the product must largely promote itself when seen alongside competing products.

- Successful diffusion of products is aided by a simple purchasing process.

- Designers sometimes need to design the physical evidence that a purchase has been made, particularly for software products.

- Aesthetic and environmental properties can be an important element of the marketing mix.

- For products to sell they need to be understood by the people selling and servicing them.

- Designs that delight the purchaser are likely to sell better and have more enduring markets than those that do not give the same pleasure.

- All products go through a life cycle of introduction, growth, maturity and decline. However the length of that cycle depends upon a number of factors.

- Purchasers that buy products at different stages of the product life cycle can be categorised as innovators, early adopters, late adopters and forced adopters.

- Different pricing strategies and marketing strategies may be used at different points of the product life cycle.

5 Designing the user experience

So far I have looked at the information that comes to design teams from the marketing department. However in some large companies and design consultancies, designers now carry out their own research with the people they are designing for.

This user-centred approach, which has been called *empathic design* by some commentators, puts the design team in direct contact with the people it is designing for. A user-centred approach to design helps designers to empathise with the potential users of the products being designed, developing the designers' understanding of users' practical circumstances and their thoughts, values and beliefs.

For many years industrial designers have attempted to consider the needs of users during the design process, often to good effect. However as purchasers have become more sophisticated in their knowledge and expectations of products, other professionals have been brought onto design teams to bring a greater understanding of psychology and culture. A design team may now involve anthropologists, ethnographers and psychologists, who advise designers from their different perspectives.

- Anthropologists study the culture and rituals of human groups.

- Ethnographers study the behaviour and cultures of people.

- Psychologists study the human mind and perceptions.

The design consultancy IDEO employs people from a wide range of backgrounds, including anthropology, psychology and biology. Similarly Philips Design employs social scientists who work alongside trained designers in product development teams and who lend their knowledge and expertise to the design process.

These social scientists are engaged in user-centred research that is carried out in several ways, including observation, detailed questioning, participant observation and self-reporting.

5.1 Observation

Observation can be carried out in three ways: observing users in their own environment, observing users while participating in an activity, or observing users in a purpose-built observation laboratory.

5.1.1 Observing people in their own environment

To find out how people use things it makes sense to go to where they are. Often this means observing people in their own homes or in the places to which they go every day.

Often by observing people at home, design teams spot workarounds or adaptations the subject has made to a product and may not even think about if they were simply describing their actions to a researcher. For example they may use their knees to prop up the washing basket as they take clothes out of a washing machine to avoid having to pick a full basket up from the floor, or they may have added string to a handle to make it easier to hold or hang up.

Research of this kind, observing people in their own environment so that the context of their actions can be seen and understood, is called *ethnographic research*. Sometimes video cameras are used to record the research – this is known as video-ethnography.

Case study | Observation at IDEO

When a team from design consultancy IDEO was asked to design a way of dispensing controlled doses of insulin to diabetics that could be used by the patients in their own homes, the team wanted to find out more. Researchers were asked to find someone with insulin-dependent diabetes who was prepared to be observed during the course of a day. The person chosen was a young woman with children.

The design team member who spent the day with her recorded the woman's day in pictures and in words. The observer watched her taking insulin in and out of the fridge, planning her day so that she would be home when she needed to take the next dose or taking the phials with her and having to ask her hosts to refrigerate them. The observer asked the subject to explain why she was doing things, observing body language and emotion in her voice as she talked about her day, adding to an understanding of how she felt about her current treatment.

On return to the office, these observations were shared with the other members of the design team, and were then fed into the creative process. The outcome of the design team's work was a single-dose insulin 'pen' that could be stored for up to 28 days without need for refrigeration, enabling diabetics to carry the supply they needed around and dispose of it safely.

On a completely different project, an IDEO team was asked to design the service on a new high-speed rail link for Amtrak, the intercity passenger train system in the United States of America. To understand the experience of passengers, and to develop a direction for the project, the design team used the trains, spent time in the stations and interviewed people. In addition designers attempted tasks like using a ticket machine while wearing gloves or in windy conditions.

The team's immersion in the experience helped it to identify 10 stages in a journey: learning, planning, starting, entering, ticketing, waiting, boarding, riding, arriving and continuing. These stages formed a framework for the team's thinking as it worked on different aspects of the new rail link.

The outcome of the design process was a set of recommendations about things that would affect the whole passenger experience, from branding through to new trains and station environments.

5.1.2 Participant observation

The example of the Amtrak project shows the IDEO team acting as participant observers. Participant observation has been used in a wide range of industries, from car design through to healthcare, as a way of understanding the experience of potential users of the product or system. Designers using this method have to be aware of their own subjectivity and familiarity with the object or system.

The Amtrak example shows how designers as participant observers try to simulate the experiences of the less able, in this case wearing gloves to use a ticket machine. Various tools have been designed to help designers to simulate the experience of disabled or elderly users – for example gloves that simulate the experience of arthritic hands to test controls and interfaces, and a whole-body suit designed to help car designers to simulate the experience of the elderly by restricting their joint movements.

You can find out more about the methods used at IDEO by watching the video on the T211 DVD.

5.1.3 Observing people in a usability laboratory

On some design projects it is useful to bring together a group of users to observe them handling products or prototypes and ask them about this experience. Philips Design, a company within the Royal Philips Electronics group, is renowned for its pioneering research with users. In its headquarters at Eindhoven in the Netherlands the company has a purpose-built *usability lab*.

The lab is a large, comfortable room with many cameras located unobtrusively on the ceiling and walls. Next to the main room is an observation suite. Here designers can watch the activity in the laboratory through a one-way mirror. They can also observe detailed behaviour on a bank of television screens that show the views from individual cameras.

This approach was used when Philips Design were looking at the possibilities of designing a handheld PDA-type computer for children. The design team gave children existing handheld computers that recognised handwriting (Apple Newtons) and asked them to participate in activities using Post-it notes to simulate the sending of messages.

By closely observing the group of children and questioning them as they played with the computers, the designers developed a feel for the ways this technology might be used and the age range for which it might be appropriate. The findings showed that a handheld computer for young people should be targeted at those aged 12 and above. The research also identified the attributes and features that such a device should have.

You can see how the usability lab at Philips Design is used in the video 'The usability lab', which is associated with this block on the T307 DVD.

5.1.4 Detailed questioning

Detailed questioning is often used alongside observation to clarify the designers' understanding and to find out more about how users feel about the products they are handling. The interviewer asks layer upon layer of questions. Here is an example of part of an exchange that might take place about setting an alarm clock:

When do you set your alarm clock? *Before I go to bed.*

Is that immediately before you go to bed? *Yes pretty much.*

Are you actually in bed when you set it? *Not quite, I usually do it before I go to the bathroom.*

Where are you when you set it? *Sometimes I sit on the bed, other times I stand up.*

How do you see to do this? *I usually have the bedside lamp on.*

Tell me what you have to do to set your alarm clock.

Such probing questions may stimulate a number of ideas, as responses to different problems or issues are raised. One example might be having a clock that lights up when it is picked up so that it can be set in the dark.

Exercise 16 User-centred design

Read the article below by Alison Black. It discusses the value of using observation and other user-centred techniques as part of the design process and shows some of the reasons why this approach is adopted, as well as some of the challenges it presents.

Black is a psychologist who specialises in developing user-focused products and services. She is consulted by design agencies, technology companies and public sector organisations.

Consider what Black means by saying that, 'if research becomes a formalised part of the design process there is a risk that its actual influence could be diminished'.

User-centred design

Alison Black

User-centred design is also known as contextual inquiry, customer-focused design, empathic design, participatory design, usability, usability engineering, usability testing, user-experience design (UXD), user-focused design and user-friendly design.

The basis of user-centred design

The central premise of user-centred design is that the best-designed products and services result from understanding the needs of the people who will use them. User-centred designers engage actively with end users to gather insights that drive design from the earliest stages of product and service development, right through the design process.

A user-centred approach can generate new insights in all design projects but it is particularly useful when a new product or service is to be introduced or where a step-change in an existing product or service is required. Awareness of the experience of end users can lead designers to question established practices and assumptions. And it can yield innovation that delivers real users benefit.

While most designers are conscious of the need to design for end users, they often base their understanding of users on their own experience or on findings from market research. In contrast, user-centred designers engage with potential users directly, believing that understanding the details of individuals' experience gives greater insight than the aggregated reports of market research, and that what people tell market researchers they do doesn't always tally with what they actually do when observed in their own context.

Many design projects involve customer or user feedback in the latter stages of concept development. But user-centred designers start engaging with users during the early, formative stages to set the agenda for their projects, rather than waiting until it may be too late to make significant changes.

User observation and analysis

User observation is based on ethnographic methods, the designer immerses him or herself in the users' context (for example spending time with users as they go about relevant tasks at work or home), usually asking open-ended questions, directed at both the practical aspects of people's tasks and the social and emotional significance they have.

Immersion in context is critical to user-centred design; it exposes unexpressed needs that would be impossible to pick up without the full context. Where products and services are to be used by groups of people cooperating (for example nurse and patient or groups of team workers), the full dynamic of their interactions can be appreciated through observation.

Observational research needs to be analysed in order to draw out key themes to be taken forward into design. It is usually recorded visually (either video or stills) so that highlights can be presented back to design teams and form the basis for idea development. The clearer the analysis and more vivid the presentation, the more likely it is to make an impact on the design team and shape product or service development.

Prototyping, evaluation and iteration

As design ideas and concepts develop, user-centred designers continue gathering input from end users, either involving them directly in design development or showing them prototypes based on their ideas for evaluation. According to the project and concept being developed, prototypes can vary from written scenarios and sketches showing broad functionality, through paper- or screen-based prototypes, to fully working models that represent full functionality.

Depending on the level of development of the prototypes, users can be asked to 'walk through' them as if they were carrying out a task, or use them to carry out simulated or real-life tasks. These prototypes provide opportunities for feedback both on the general fit of the product or service to people's needs and on its step-by-step usability.

As with observation, the feedback from prototype evaluation needs to be analysed and its results taken forward into design thinking as part of an interactive process of designing and evaluating.

Representing the full range of user need

The purpose of user research in design is to inspire and focus the design team rather than gather quantitative data (although a quantitative approach may be appropriate at the final stages of testing usability). When time and budget are constrained, the emphasis should be to gather input from the widest range of users possible (most products and services have different kinds of users). This should mean that the full potential is understood, rather than carrying out repeat observations or evaluations with the same kind of user.

Why it matters to business

User focus in design increases competitiveness, leading to the development of products and services that people:

- genuinely need and value
- find intuitive and easy to use.

Company reputations and customer loyalty are built by positive user experiences. In web-based services, in particular, it is very easy for people to 'click' to an alternative website if a service doesn't meet their needs.

A user-centred approach broadens the scope of inputs to designers' thinking. Design teams are often physically and culturally removed from the people they design for. Over the course of product and service development, designers, engineers, planners and marketeers can grow so close to the concepts and technologies they are developing that their expectations don't match those of everyday end users. Those who take pains to understand the context they are designing for and who include users' perspectives in the evaluation of their work have a greater chance of business success.

A user-centred approach to product and service development provides a unifying framework for organisational strategy. It brings the interests of different departments such as research, operations and marketing together, generating a coherent development strategy and reducing the wastage of conflicting initiatives. Relatively small investments in user research from the earliest stages of development can help set the agenda for product and service development.

Why it matters to public services

The public services have long been caricatured as insensitive to the needs of their users. Because user-centred design draws together the practical, emotional and social aspects of people's experience it is an ideal basis for developing innovative service concepts. A user-centred approach is in keeping with Government intentions to provide services that respond to the needs of individuals and to present 'joined-up' solutions working across different Government departments.

Planning strategies that are not based on an understanding of user need and capability are likely to perpetuate both public hostility and poor uptake of services. User-centred design will enable cost-effective development, trial and evolution of new services before full-scale launch. Because the results of such a process are focused on user need and capability they should not be prone to user errors (both by the public and by service deliverers) and the inefficiencies and expense resulting from those errors.

Where the political agenda drives innovation, user-centred design can pinpoint the consequences for specific user groups and allow preparation of an appropriate response. Such an approach could, for example, have mitigated the 'digital divide' that has developed in the UK and seems likely to limit uptake of online service delivery (e-government).

User-centred design needs to be sensitive to the complexity of public-service administration and the severe budgetary constraints upon it. Within this context, user-centred design helps to find routes that maximise the impact of service development – both in the number and range of people included. Design that is responsive to the wide range of user needs should increase the inclusivity of public services (for example schools and hospitals) and discourage the opting out that works to their detriment.

Challenges

The interplay between observational user research and market research

User research may at first sight seem unnecessary where there is pre-existing market research showing people's expressed preferences and needs. Market research usually entails interviews with groups of representative people, so is often thought of as 'valid' because of the force of numbers behind it. In contrast, it is the detailed and often unexpected insights that come from contact with individual users that inspire design. It is likely to be more important for designers to observe a range of different users rather than large numbers of 'typical' users.

There will be overlap between the findings of market research and user observation. But once it is accepted that the goals of market research and user research are distinct it should be uncontroversial to make a case for targeted, observational research that is well integrated into the design process.

Using expert review rather than evaluation with end users

Many designers (particularly in software development) promote expert review of concept prototypes rather than testing them with end users. While usability experts can pinpoint flaws in newly developed products and services their perspective is not that of end users and important problems may be missed. Expert review is promoted as a cost-effective ('discount') evaluation technique.

However failure to detect problems for users may result in more cost than the expense of user testing, albeit deferred beyond the development process. Expert review can be particularly inappropriate for web applications where the range of users and their interests and goals is diverse.

Nevertheless, if user testing is not possible for confidentiality reasons, expert review is a potential alternative. Where budget is constrained, a combination of expert review and testing a small, diverse set of users may reduce costs.

Producing 'valid' research – who to observe or test?

Since the object of design research is rarely to produce statistically valid data, the focus of recruitment for user research should be on gathering insights from a diverse group of potential users. It makes sense to map out the range of people likely to be using a new product or service and aim to get coverage across the range. Extreme users can sometimes give value to the rest of the population.

Recruitment is frequently a problem in user research but the quality of the research depends upon targeting the right people. Despite setting detailed criteria for research recruiters you may find they deliver research participants who only partially meet your criteria.

Recruitment via personal connections may yield better results. Newspaper advertisements and notices to relevant organisations, clubs or special interest groups may help. Allow time for recruitment and be prepared for the expense of placing advertisements and paying recruitment fees.

Producing 'valid' research – how many to observe or test?

The aim of observation is coverage of a wide range of users, rather than producing statistically valid data. So it is a good idea to observe enough people in different contexts to feel confident that you have understood the scope of potential need. The point where you find you are getting repetition from observations is probably the point to stop.

In concept testing, again, you need to ensure coverage of the significant potential users of products and services.

There has been debate about the number of people needed to test basic usability of products and services. Research in both traditional product development and in the development of software tools suggests that the majority of usability problems emerge after testing with five to seven people. However, complex products and services with diverse functionality will need more extensive evaluation programmes.

Maintaining the impact of research findings within the design programme

In large-scale or extended design projects the impact of user research may be lost because not all designers have had the opportunity to participate in the research or simply because time has intervened since the research was carried out.

Once research has been undertaken, effort is needed to analyse it and communicate it to the rest of the design team. Workshops involving the whole design team, to present the findings visually and to draw out the implications for the project, help keep focus on the research base.

Written research reports tend to be filed and ignored. Techniques to maintain the impact of research include:

- keeping research findings graphic and visual

- creating a project space in which the research and implications are displayed

- developing fictitious characters that have the characteristics of people who have been observed and using them as players in illustrated scenarios where future products and services are used.

Future trends

Mainstreaming of a user-centred approach

Since the 1980s, user-centred design has gained influence and most designers now claim to be user-centred or to carry out user research. This may simply mean testing design solutions in the latter stages of design projects but there is increasing understanding of the need for research in the early stages of a project in order to inspire design. Many design courses now include introductions to user research so newly qualified designers should be increasingly aware of its benefits.

Adoption of observational research in market research

Market research agencies, many of whom have previously dismissed user research (especially ethnographic research) as not having adequate coverage, are now including it in their repertoire of techniques.

New research techniques to inspire design

User-centred designers are concerned to increase the effectiveness of their research and to develop techniques that are appropriate to design development. The cultural-probe research techniques, first used by Bill Gaver and Tony Dunne at the Royal College of Art in the 1990s and still under development, are gaining influence in design research. These techniques encourage people to express thoughts and emotions that might not be revealed through standard observation, but that may be highly inspirational for design work.

Ensuring research relevance and integration

As user research becomes mainstream within design there will be a need for clarity about what research is being done, what its goals are and how its outcomes are integrated into subsequent design. User research usually has most impact when research and design processes are enmeshed. However, if research becomes a formalised part of the design process there is a risk that its actual influence could be diminished.

(Source: Black, undated)

Discussion

My understanding of what Alison Black says is that the value of user-centred design lies in the designer's engagement with that research. If user research simply becomes a formal hoop to be jumped through by the design team there is a danger the information gleaned will not be embraced in the same way as it is when the motivation for user research comes from the design team itself.

SAQ 19

What advantages does a user-centred approach to design have over conventional market research techniques?

SAQ 20

How can the results of user-centred research be brought into the design process?

5.2 Other user-centred techniques adopted by designers

In addition to the observation techniques discussed above, a number of other approaches can be found in innovative design practices. Some of these are explained briefly below.

5.2.1 Bodystorming

Bodystorming is a form of creative role-play in which designers act out the use of a potential product. This may involve props, for example a rough mock-up of the product made out of simple materials such as card, paper and tape. Alternatively someone may take on the role of the product while someone else takes on the role of the user to explore the interaction between a user and the potential product.

For example, to explore the potential features of a new clock, a dialogue between 'clock' and 'user' might take place. Acting out the scenario in a creative atmosphere can throw up many ideas about the interface that may not have emerged from more conventional techniques.

5.2.2 Cultural probes

Cultural probes for finding out about the aspirations and attitudes of different cultural groups were devised by staff at the Royal College of Art in London. The techniques use creative ways of asking users to reveal information about themselves, such as giving people stickers to show how they would like to spend their money or to indicate how they feel about different areas of their homes or community. The project described below offers an insight into how these techniques have been used with communities in three European countries.

Case study | Presence project

The Presence Project brought together a wide range of organisations, including the Helen Hamlyn Centre at the Royal College of Art. The project aimed to develop new ways for ordinary people, especially older people, to interact with computers and the internet so that they could access information for themselves and reduce their dependency on welfare services. Based on three test sites in different countries (Italy, Norway and the Netherlands) the project used both low-tech and cutting-edge technologies in the research.

The method used by designers of the project was a form of design-led user study known as cultural probes. This method was used to probe older people's lives and attitudes. The designers then used conceptual proposals for innovative services and systems to design experiments, and later tested working prototypes in the communities they were working with.

Cultural probes

From the beginning of the project the design teams were aware that each of the three sites had its own identity, physical setting and culture and that the personalities of the participating older people were different. The designers decided to respond to each community separately.

The design teams needed to understand the three communities in depth but had neither the time for a lengthy ethnographic study nor the budget for more traditional methods, such as questionnaire studies or focus groups. In any case the outcome of these more traditional methods would have been too impersonal to give the designers the empathic understanding they required. The team therefore decided on the use of cultural probes to explore the design issues.

Approximately 10 cultural probe packages were prepared for each of the three sites, tailored to the individual communities. Each contained maps, postcards, a disposable camera, a media diary and even an egg timer, all designed to prompt responses and discover participants' habits and emotional, aesthetic and social values (Figure 37).

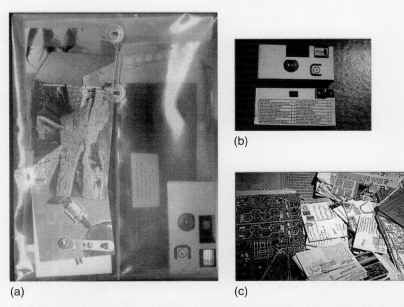

(a)   (b)   (c)

Figure 37   (a) One of the cultural probe packs. (b) Disposable camera with prompts printed on the back, saying such things as 'your home', 'something ugly', 'something beautiful'. (c) Pile of responses showing the quantity and richness of data collected. Source: Gaver (1996)

Postcards combined open-ended questions with evocative images to invite discussion. Postcards were used because most people associate them with an informal, casual writing style. The cards allowed the designers to ask a wide range of questions in a relaxed way, such as 'What advice or insight has influenced you?' 'What is your favourite device?' and even 'What use are politicians?'.

Maps were also included in each package, printed on the backs of envelopes. The designers asked the older people to indicate the emotional topography of their communities – in other words local landmarks that held meaning for them, places where their friends lived, places they found intriguing or dangerous, and so on. The participants indicated these places with the stickers they had been given – some coloured, some printed with images.

The packages also included a disposable *camera*, which had been repackaged in an outer sleeve to link it with the other materials. A variety of requests were printed on the back of the camera, asking the participants to take pictures such as the view from their window, the clothes they would wear that day and things they found beautiful, ugly, desirable or boring. The groups were asked to use any remaining film simply to take pictures of things they thought would help the researchers to know them better, giving them the freedom to choose what the designers could see.

In addition to all of the items discussed above, the users were given a *media diary* in which they were asked to make a record of all the television programmes they watched and radio programmes they listened to.

Phase 1

When the cultural probe packs had been created, the designers held meetings at each site. These meetings lasted 2 hours, and at each meeting the designers gave out the cultural probe packs to the local groups. The designers stressed to participants the collaborative and experimental nature of the materials and asked for the residents' help and suggestions.

At each site participants responded enthusiastically, eagerly opening and exploring the packages. The ensuing discussions were lively and very informative. Most participants returned most materials within a couple of weeks, furnishing the design centres with around 120 maps, 200 cards, 500 photographs and 25 media diaries.

There was no attempt at a rigorous quantitative analysis – the probes were explicitly not designed to support this – but rather to draw out patterns and exceptions. Even in their raw state the probes served as inspirational materials for members of the project. The methodology was seen as an exciting and effective way to open a two-way dialogue.

Phase 2

In the second phase of the project the design team generated a wide range of proposals for each of the three sites. The items from the cultural probes study were used, in conjunction with photographs, anecdotes and souvenirs from visits to the sites, to inspire ideas for a wide variety of systems that might be developed further. The ideas generated were recorded for discussion with partner organisations and the participants at each of the sites.

A structured workbook was made, using a variety of imagery to create storyboards of the proposed systems, using descriptive text to provide a framework and organisation for the ideas. These workbooks were presented to the participants in each of the sites during visits. The aim was to encourage them to respond to the designers' ideas for possible systems through feedback and generating further ideas.

The discussion of the workbook with the users and partner organisations led to firm design proposals for each site. An interactive multimedia presentation of the design proposals was created. Separate screens described each community to set the context for the proposals, and animated diagrams of the systems being suggested were presented along with a 'catalogue of parts' showing the kinds of physical artefacts that might make up the systems.

Phase 3
Design experiments

The next step was to build and test mock-ups of the systems in the three sites. The design team used low-tech means to simulate the systems and test the proposals, assessing aesthetics, social effects and cultural implications. In the course of the experiments it became clear the technical concerns and intellectual challenges offered by the proposed systems would play a large role in deciding which to take forward.

Phase 4
Working prototypes

The design experiments at the three sites took longer than expected and it became obvious it would be too difficult to create three different working systems. The design team decided to develop and test the system it had designed for Bijlmer in Amsterdam. This decision was made because the earlier experiment had worked best there and the local community was enthusiastic. The team was also intrigued by the complexity of this area and wanted to pursue the ideas that it had inspired.

Outcomes

The designers developed interfaces and created scenarios about the communications infrastructure in the communities with which they worked. The interfaces that were developed during the course of the project were designed to be aesthetic, a pleasure to use and to work well. The interfaces also had to be multimodal to allow people of different abilities to use them on different devices.

The resulting designs included the incorporation of input and output devices 'hidden' in the environment of public spaces or homes. One of the outcomes was the design of a bench in which messages could be displayed. The elderly participants had identified a concern for their safety and a need to communicate with younger members of the community in Bijlmer. The bench was conceived as a way to enable this communication.

However the project ended at this stage and the ideas arising from it have yet to be permanently implemented. Nevertheless the project gave the designers a better understanding of what to consider when designing information technology products and services for older people and people with different needs.

Perhaps the main importance of this project was that it led to the development of the cultural probe methodology for exploring user needs – this has subsequently been used by other designers in their own design work.

5.2.3 Changes after the product launch

A user-centred approach means that feedback will be gathered and acted upon even after a product has been launched. The process is iterative – feedback leads to changes, which in turn lead to product improvements and developments. As well as incremental improvements it is even possible for user feedback to stimulate radically new ideas for completely new product solutions. Complex technical products often go through many iterations, some driven by user feedback and some by developments in technology.

It is possible for companies to respond to user feedback without adopting a truly user-centred approach. Many companies respond to feedback on quality or safety, or even good suggestions, without necessarily placing the user at the centre of the redesign process. When a user-centred approach is adopted, proposed changes will be discussed with, and tested by, users before new products are launched onto the market.

5.2.4 Inclusive design

A growing number of designers are now concerned with using inclusive design when conceiving and developing products. *Inclusive design* is design that considers users with disabilities and seeks to create products that can be used by them, as well as by other users.

Frequently changes to a product that benefit disabled users also benefit able-bodied users. In addition to the use of observation and user-centred techniques to understand the needs of the disabled user, products have been developed to simulate the user experience for the designer.

The gloves that were mentioned briefly in the discussion of participant observation were designed by a research group in Cambridge to simulate the experience of impaired manual dexterity by users such as elderly people with arthritic hands. To test the simulation gloves against the experience of disabled users, the researchers set up an experiment in conjunction with a testing house. Users were asked to try to set a number of central heating controllers. This experiment showed that simulation tools could help designers to predict with reasonably accuracy where problems may occur.

However the involvement of disabled users in the design process might identify problems or generate far more ideas than could be achieved using simulation alone. Listening to users talk about their whole experience of the product under test, rather than focusing solely on the physical aspects of use, can provide unexpected and useful insights for the designer.

 The Helen Hamlyn Research Centre at the Royal College of Art focuses on developing inclusive designs. Some examples of this centre's work can be seen on the T211 DVD. Read the case study below to get an insight into how user-centred, inclusive design has been used to redesign a shower for a European manufacturer.

Case study Improving the shower for old people

Methodology

A Helen Hamlyn research associate began the project with a market analysis of existing bathroom products. A questionnaire was sent to 100 people from various social backgrounds to establish different bathing techniques and relaxation preferences. Of this sample, 60 were older people, while the rest were younger people, including some with young children. Home visits were also made during this period and each user was interviewed about their bathroom and their specific bathing habits. From this study general problem areas were isolated for further discussion.

A focus group of 13 older people then identified four specific problems that they face in the bathroom, especially when showering: drying after bathing, reaching for the soap, adjusting the shower handset and balancing to avoid slipping.

The problem areas generated a series of design proposals, which were further tested with four older users (Figure 38), each of whom had severely reduced mobility and therefore represented some extreme problems the older market experiences. This user group was consulted at various stages of the design and development process to give direct feedback on ideas and prototypes.

Figure 38   Bill, one of the participants in the user research
Source: Helen Hamlyn Research Centre

Issues

The project identified four key areas of concern in showering for older people.

1   *Drying after bathing.* Most people did not want to step out of the bath or shower while wet because of the possibility of slipping on a wet surface. They also found it difficult to reach certain parts of the body to dry because of immobility, stiffness or reduced dexterity.

2   *Reaching for the soap.* While standing in the bath or shower, soap and shower gel were often difficult to reach and use with wet hands. These difficulties led to a number of concerns, such as strains from stretching, slipping while unbalanced and disorientation.

3   *Not being able to move the shower handset.* One of the problems many people found as they became older was their inability to reposition the actual handset of the shower in its wall cradle or bar. A fear of overbalancing while stretching made the shower facility unsafe for many users.

4   *Fears about safety.* Most older users felt that a shower was neither safe nor relaxing. They saw the qualities of a bath – reclining, bubble bath, head support, reduced risk of slipping – as being far more relaxing and safer than a shower.

Results

Two central design concepts emerged from the study. The first incorporates a warm air drier, showerhead soap dispenser and reclining shower seat within a single, integrated luxury shower unit. The second replaces traditional bathroom fittings with a series of tiles, including magnetic tiles that allow easy adjustment of the shower handset, tap tiles activated by hand pressure and shower tiles creating a gentle cascade of water through body jets (Figure 39).

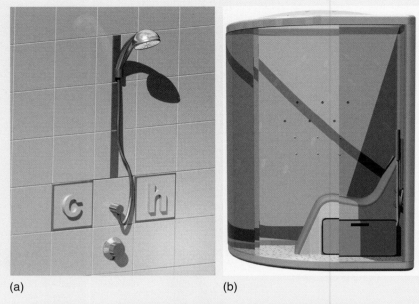

(a)   (b)

Figure 39 (a) Prototype shower showing the touch-sensitive tiles for cold and hot water. (b) Concept for a shower cubicle. Source: Helen Hamlyn Research Centre

The design process behind these proposals was captured in a special publication for shower manufacturer Hansgrohe, entitled *Waterfall*. Hansgrohe went on to explore the development of these concepts for manufacture in collaboration with the research associate.

The project addressed the research issues in a particular way that was inclusive of all user needs. But many other possible solutions exist. Can looking at bathing and hygiene from other cultures, such as Asian wet rooms, bring a fresh approach to design? Can listening to users help designers and bathroom manufacturers to address the needs of older consumers in an inclusive rather than stigmatising manner?

5.2.5 Role of the testing house

Not all companies desire, or can afford, to carry out extensive work with users in-house. However there are testing houses that can be commissioned by manufacturers to do this work for them. When a testing house is used, the results obtained are passed to the commissioning company. This report or its main findings will be passed on to the design and production departments, who will then consider necessary improvements or developments.

The work of many testing houses focuses on safety and performance factors but there are a few testing houses around the world which specialise in working with users to gather information about their qualitative experiences.

Case study | Product testing and certification

The Intertek ETL Semko testing house in Milton Keynes used to belong to the UK Consumers' Association but is now part of a global group of testing houses whose motto is, 'Testing everywhere for markets anywhere'. The 'ETL' in the name shows the company's heritage as a descendant of Thomas Edison's Electrical Testing Laboratory, set up in the nineteenth century to carry out tests on product concepts and prototypes.

In the twenty-first century this company carries out a range of tests for both companies and government bodies. Some of these are physical tests performed in the laboratory and others are subjective tests with consumers and users.

Laboratory tests

The tests carried out under laboratory conditions simulate the use of products by users so that various aspects of those products can be evaluated in a rigorous and scientific way. Tests carried out have to be replicable – in other words, for consistency, the same conditions have to be able to be repeated time and time again on different products. The outcomes of almost all of these laboratory tests are quantitative, statistical data.

Performance tests. Continuous performance testing is used to simulate use over a prolonged period. For example putting a weight equivalent to a person on and off a chair, thousands of times or until the product fails.

Controlled environment tests. This form of test uses controlled environment rooms to see how performance is affected by heat, cold and humidity, for example using thermocouples embedded in food simulation packs to test for hot and cold spots in fridges and freezers under a variety of climatic conditions.

Comparative tests. These tests compare the performance of competing products using controlled experiments, for example testing the efficiency of dishwashers by using standard tests that use specified foods such as spinach painted and dried onto standard plates. The results are measured and comparisons made based on a number of criteria.

Safety tests. Products have to meet government standards and the manufacturers' own specifications so that those products can be certified as safe. For example toasters are tested by jamming pieces of toast into them to see what happens. A millimetre of plastic casing too near to the heat source could give rise to catastrophic results.

Energy tests. Testing houses are used to carry out the independent tests of products that are required by European standards to certify the energy use and rating of products, for example testing cookers to determine energy labelling. The testing house seen on the T307 DVD also plays a role in testing goods to advise the government on future policy through the Market Transformation Programme.

User tests

In addition to the rigorous testing described above, some testing houses also carry out research directly with users, yielding a mix of qualitative and quantitative data.

Panels of users. The testing house seen on the T307 DVD uses panels of users for its tests. To give some idea of the size of these panels, in 2005 it had one panel of 1000 members, who were all members of the

Consumers' Association and who were only used in trials for that organisation. It had another panel of 500 members for independent testing, and a special panel of 250 disabled members who are used to carry out testing for an organisation that campaigns on issues of disability. The number of users involved in tests will vary depending on the nature of the test. The characteristics of each panel member are known from an extensive questionnaire that is filled in as part of the application procedure to become a panel member. If the tests have been commissioned by companies, users are carefully selected from among the panel members to provide a sample that meets the manufacturers' criteria.

User tests. For some tests panel members are asked to use products in a controlled setting within the Intertek building, for example preparing a food using given ingredients to test food-processing or cooking equipment. Sometimes tests on garden equipment are conducted in open spaces and nearby parks. Although not taking place under laboratory conditions, the parameters of the test enable comparisons between products to be made under similar conditions and on similar tasks at the same time.

User trials. User trials look at the user experience in the context of their own homes. Panel members are asked to use products in their own homes or gardens for a set period to collect information about use in context and over time.

Development user tests. Tests to inform future product development may be devised and run in the testing house. For example to find out the optimum size of a taxi that would be accessible to people with all types of disabilities, a test rig was built in part of the laboratory. The rig had an adjustable door width and height, and other features to simulate a taxi. This was tested by members of the disability panel with a range of impairments.

Whichever method is used, the information on the users' experiences is collected on structured questionnaires. However alongside the structured questions there is always a column for comments, allowing open-ended feedback to be given.

The outcome of all of the tests performed at Intertek is written up in the form of a report, which is given to the commissioning organisation or company.

Sometimes, when general observations are made that may be of use to an industry as a whole, Intertek may approach industry organisations with a view to disseminating its findings and working with the industry on the improvement of product standards. For example general findings about the use of such products as mobile phones have been fed back to the relevant industry associations.

You can learn more about this testing house by watching the video 'Testing house' on the T307 DVD.

SAQ 21

What is the role of the testing house in the product design and development process?

5.3 Usability

Usability concerns the ease of use of a product. The term is frequently used in connection with interface design, particularly computer interfaces such as computer programs and websites. Because an increasing number of products are a synthesis of hardware and software, the issues of usability are as important in product design as they are in the design of computer software. Do you know how to use all of the features of your mobile phone? Can you understand the options offered by your DVD player?

The opportunities for action and interactions that objects offer are known as *affordances*. Users look at an object and perceive what they can do with it – what it affords them or provides for them.

You will have learned to 'read' objects that you have never seen before and understand the affordances they offer. For example if you look at an object with wheels you understand that it has the affordance of mobility. On your mobile phone, you have the affordances of input, display and alerting. How users relate to objects and use the opportunities they are afforded depends upon whether users can understand the design of the object and its interfaces.

Conventions have been developed to assist users in their use of objects. These standard features are created to help users to understand how to use the objects around them. Examples include the cursor arrow on a computer changing to a hand shape to show the user they can grab and move an item, and the red marker on top of a hot water tap.

The way to find out whether users can perceive all of the opportunities offered by a product, or can understand the conventions that have been designed to assist them, is to carry out usability tests with real users. This is a much less expensive way to find problems than launching a product and only finding out about the difficulties when that product is already in production.

5.4 Focus of design

Over the past few decades the focus of designers and companies has shifted towards greater emphasis on the user experience.

Exercise 17 Roles of technology and design

Read the article below, which was published by Philips Design.

The evolving roles of technology and design

Philips Design

We all know it. In the last few decades, technology has brought about dramatic changes to our life styles, and, it seems, it will carry on doing so for the time to come. Scientists, engineers and programmers are constantly at work to try to create the new gadget that will help technological companies, now competing in a market characterized by price erosion and saturation, to retain (or gain!) the competitive edge.

But how did we come to this situation? How can companies respond to the challenge of keeping leadership in the 'no needs' market? Is technology push the answer to the challenge or just a repetition of the 'old way' of doing things, which sooner or later will stop providing with the wished results? Can design play a role in all this?

The booming years

In order to answer this question, it is necessary to look at the way in which technology and its perception have changed in the last few decades.

The market for technological products has grown very fast, in many cases even exponentially. This outstanding growth, which started at the beginning of the last century but accelerated from the 1950s, was mainly driven by the desire to own an ever-increasing number of objects that could make our lives easier and more comfortable.

What, just before the Second World War, were dreams, such as automatic washing for clothes, television broadcasting, stereo sound, easy telecommunications and others, became attainable in the post-war period.

Economic growth and political stability in the Western world helped the development of a situation in which an increasing number of individuals could afford products that, only a few years beforehand, were the wonders of a restricted elite. Mass production began and, with it, the fast and overwhelming invasion of electronic products into our homes.

If, at the beginning of the nineteenth century, the first technological developments to reach people's homes (such as electricity) were greeted as wonders, the second wave of technological products, those that invaded our houses after the Second World War, were greeted in the name of comfort.

The new horizon of possibilities offered by technology fascinated people from the very start. The fact that technology was the means to achieve a better quality of life was not put under discussion. The very notion of progress started to coincide with that of technological innovation. Technology was the goddess of change, the element that would free us from manual, repetitive work and from housework, and that would enhance our quality of life by providing us with more interesting jobs, with affordable communications, with home entertainment. Every field of human activity was suddenly turning its attention to technology and greeting its development as progress.

The focus was on the function: practical convenience and maintenance, as well as hygiene, were the qualities that people were looking for in their appliances and equipment. Possible improvements for the new ranges were better performance or safety.

Technology and functionality attracted consumers to the purchase, with other elements, such as design or brand reputation, as secondary. Technology was therefore dictating to marketing and even to styling, as that had to reflect the values that consumers were after (again, hygiene, performance and ease of maintenance).

Towards market saturation

As quantity, and thus mass production and consumption, were the conditions to continue on the growth path, it soon appeared clear that, sooner or later, market saturation was going to appear at the horizon and to start threatening the new wealth and development.

Once the market was saturated in any part of the world it was obvious that there would be a shift in the push to the purchase. What was previously perceived as a new attractive element was bound to become simply an implicit quality. Whatever had been driving the market so far (just the attractiveness of buying devices that would make our lives easier and more comfortable) was no longer enough in a situation in which everyone owned at least one of these devices already.

Companies and brands started therefore to concentrate efforts in the pursuit of new value propositions that would ensure continuous growth. They acted on two fronts: technological and geographical expansion.

They invested in researching technologies that would allow new functionalities to be proposed in the new generations of products. Electronic products were perceived as items to use, thus objects whose purpose was to perform a certain task. The more the tasks, the more attractive the product would be for the consumers. This worked very well for quite a long time, until it became clear that adding too many functionalities on a product was actually counterproductive. The usability of such a product was in fact becoming so complicated as to make the extra function totally useless.

The other weapon that companies and brands were using to face up to market saturation was the enlargement of the markets themselves. The products that had an already very high penetration in Western countries had reached such maturity and low prices (due to the mass production) that they could now be sold to other countries, thus fuelling once again the corporate wallets.

Through this 'unarmed colonisation' electronic goods and Western lifestyle have invaded the homes of a vast amount of the world population (although some countries are still not reached), achieving an amazing degree of penetration. The situation is such that nowadays more and more consumers can afford and enjoy these electronic functional benefits, especially those relating to information, communication and entertainment.

Yet, it is actually due to its great success that technology has now become almost a commodity, and market saturation is now a certain reality.

Some technologies (such as telecommunications, video and audio functionalities, kitchen appliances and so on) have reached such a level of penetration that consumers have come to take *any* functional benefits for granted.

With the commoditization of such electronic products and market saturation, price erosion has also emerged. The value consumers place on these commodity products has declined, and the value of the market itself is declining. What a company could ask for a certain product a year ago is more than what it can ask for today.

The outcome is the fierce global competition that confronts electronics brands today. As they compete to grow – or even just maintain some semblance of market share and profitability – companies have often chosen to cut prices and reduce margins as new ways to achieve their targets. This is obviously another way to carry on doing business in the old way, rather than focussing on finding a new solution.

The search for new value

In the last few years, many companies and brands have finally started to feel the strong need to find the new attractive qualities that will create new interest in the consumers' arena and that will bring companies back to profitability.

The development of new digital technologies and products has revamped the industry through a new technology push. If we look at the field of one of the most commoditized products, such as a TV set, we see that until the early nineties the focus was still on picture quality and sound on the old CRT screens. Then, slowly, the industry started investing in new areas such as digital TV, digital recording and DVDs, flat panel displays, home cinema experience and so forth. But the speed through which the new technologies were accepted by the consumers, and through which new inventions were picked up by the competition (which, not having to recover for the research investments could offer far lower prices) were fuelling the price erosion. The rate of creation of new digital inventions became so fast that it was difficult for consumers to keep up. All this made it clear that focusing solely on the development of new technologies was not a long-term answer.

Of course technological innovations continue to create value, but they're no longer the sole qualities that persuade consumers to purchase electronic products. Rather, people are experiencing some sort of confusion in front of the ever-increasing amount of gadgets and functionalities that they are faced with.

The new role of technology

What has truly changed is the role that technology plays in people's lives: first wonder, then comfort carrier, now technology is a way of being. Everyone wants it, and to the highest possible degree of sophistication. Being 'high tech' is somewhat a primary necessity, just as eating bread or drinking water. It is no longer something special, a new attractive quality that could, alone, inspire consumers to the purchase. It's got to be there, and at the highest level of performance, but something extra needs to be offered to differentiate one's product from the thousands of others that feature the same performance and functionalities.

The new aspirational values and the new role of design

But the complexity of today's situation goes far beyond market saturation and price erosion. The socio-cultural arena has also dramatically changed in the last few years, with new paradigms and life styles now set for new generations that are increasingly difficult to pinpoint.

When, approximately in the 1980s, functionality of products in itself stopped being the attractive quality that would push consumers to the purchase, companies started to come out with new propositions in communications that suggested products could satisfy new, emerging needs. Clearly, people no longer needed a television, a radio or a telephone, as they already had it all. The most advanced marketers started therefore marketing the 'dreams' that certain products could allow people to experience, thus glorifying possession in itself rather than the actual use, which was taken for granted. In other words, functional values had been replaced by aspirational values, life style propositions that were able to attract the new generation of consumers who had never experienced the 'needs' society.

Examples of great success stories in the 'sale of dreams' are seen in brands such as Alessi, or Swatch. These brands clearly do not sell the function of their products but the emotional impact that the object would have in the user's life and in illustrating his personality to the outside world. This approach, which nowadays has become almost mainstream and is applied to all sorts of products, was quite revolutionary in the 1980s.

From that moment onwards, design started to appear on the horizon as a possible new attractive quality.

Could design replace technology as the new attractive quality for consumers? Were consumers ready to pay more for products that would carry the same functions but that looked more attractive and that were able to create a more meaningful emotional bond?

One of the first attempts to bring attractive design to technological products for mass manufacture occurred with the launch of the Philips-Alessi line of domestic appliances in 1994.

Philips and Alessi

With the slogan 'restoring the balance', this range of kitchen appliances brought a more human face to technology in use in the home. Like a Manifesto, the Philips-Alessi line not only indicated a new style direction (style is ephemeral) but a new approach to technology in the domestic life style, focusing on restoring the values of Affection and Rituality in the home. Soft, pastel colours were used instead of the traditional white, whilst a sturdy, enhanced polypropylene (that resembled the bakelite used in the historical appliances) was selected to allow thicker wall sections, thus increasing stability. Both the colours and the material were carriers of the message: technology can be friendly, technology is not to be hidden, and technology is human.

The success of the range (the products are now collectors' items) proved that it was possible, for a large multinational, to follow the logic of the small, family driven company and to pursue quality rather than quantity in the search for new, long-term profitability.

After the Philips-Alessi range, the world of domestic appliances was no longer the same. All of a sudden, design became the 'in' word and retailers were flooded with colourful, personalized objects, aimed at our kitchens.

Design was the new attractive quality but, in most cases, it was simply applied as a sort of mascara on top of existing propositions, rather than as a tool to stimulate the creation of a new approach of product ranges (as it had been with Philips-Alessi).

Design, as styling, was comparatively cheap to have, it did not require expensive research budgets and it could be used to enhance the attractiveness of products that otherwise, from the technical point of view, had nothing left to say.

This wave of colour and personality quickly spread to other segments, such as TVs and even office appliances until the point that design is now everywhere, its attractiveness fading away fast.

The evolution of design

But design is far more than just styling. Not only the aesthetics of design have evolved in the last years, but the very meaning of the interaction between people and technology has changed, and thus has design. The more complex the function, the more designers had an important role to play, that went far beyond styling. Therefore also their contribution to the creation of the new attractive quality can go far beyond styling.

The evolution of interaction design illustrates this added value very clearly. In the past, functionality was simple and immediately clear to the user. This was also facilitated by the fact that the visual appearance of the new appliances usually followed that of their predecessors. Electric kettles, for example, looked just like gas kettles; the difference was that instead of being placed on top of burning gas, they only needed to be plugged into an electrical current. In this way, an 'intuitive relationship' was automatically established between people and the 'new objects'.

As the years passed, and new machines and technologies were developed, providing a whole new range of applications, the relationship between people and technology started to become more complex. The functionality of these new objects was no longer linked to their form. There was no 'anthropological' reference to consider when designing a computer; it was an object capable of performing totally 'new' tasks and there were no models for its behaviour. Consequently the form, the language, the interaction between man and this new machine were all driven by the needs of the machine, not its user. So these 'new intelligent objects' became the domain of a few adepts, people capable of communicating with them through special codes, a language, in fact, that was machine-oriented rather than user-oriented. Design became simply the 'box' that was wrapping the product, rather than a core element in its development, as the focus was totally on the technology.

Slowly, over the last thirty years, more 'human' interactions and designs have been created. If we look at the development of interactions between man and the machine, we see a pattern, one that takes us from a machine-focused interaction towards an increasingly intuitive, natural interaction, one that makes use of our bodily gestures or of objects that are, once again, anthropologically meaningful. This was the case with the Philips-Alessi line but more examples can be drawn out in the area of interaction design.

The first significant change in the man-machine interaction came with the introduction of icons. After that, multimedia added value not just for vision but also for hearing and touch. Later, 'agent technology' enabled the creation of environments responsive to multiple users while, more recently still, virtual reality tools have introduced us to the concept of simulated environments.

Ultimately, the path is towards making the interaction so natural that we will not even realize that we are using technology. Technology will be invisible, integrated into our environment.

And, with technology progressively diffused around us, and increasingly able to address not just our physical senses but even time, we will no longer think of product, software or interface design: we will think of 'design of the experience'.

Design of the experience

It is with this idea in mind that Philips Design has been concentrating its research activities on experience design.

The Philips Design approach is guided by high design: a philosophy founded on the idea that only anthropologically relevant solutions will be ultimately successful not only for the short but also for the long-term. High design is a design process in which expertise from the human sciences, technology, marketing are fused together in a research-based approach, that aims at identifying solutions that are technologically possible, but also humanly preferable.

Experience design is one of the core elements of high design. It focuses on the quality of the user experience during the whole period of engagement with a product; from the first impression and the feeling of discovery, through aspects of usability, cultural relevance and durability, to the memory of the complete relationship. This puts users firmly at the centre of the design process, with their input and feedback being integrated throughout the whole design process and product life-cycle.

Experience design incorporates many different disciplines to achieve this, including socio-cultural research, product design, e-design, and visual/graphic design. Its multifaceted process begins with an analysis of current trends in technology, environment, design and other relevant issues. This is augmented by cultural scans and analysis of change in personal, domestic, public and mobile environments worldwide. A workshop follows to generate scenarios and create concepts based on the most promising ideas. After filtering, the conclusions are used to draw out a roadmap, which defines what can be done in the short-, medium- and long-term. Prototypes of the products and technologies are created, based on these guidelines and then tested among a wide cross section of the user group. Their initial impressions, their assessment of how intuitive the product is to use, and their opinion on other issues such as social relevance are carefully noted, with the results implemented and presented again.

This iterative design methodology makes the end result far more human-focused because it fully embraces so many different aspects of user opinion. It also ensures that technology, although obviously instrumental in determining the functionality, is no longer the driver. In fact, people shouldn't be expected to learn technical skills in order to access new, advanced functionality. Rather, technology should be considered to be the enabler of greater simplicity, elegance and pleasure in people's day-to-day lives.

Experience design involves discussions with technologists, manufacturers and business managers in order to determine the optimal approach to manufacturing and supporting products, services and environments.

The purpose of all the experience design projects is not to define 'standard' experiences for people to have, and its approach is totally different from that of software design of games for instance. Its purpose is to design multisensory stimuli from which people could create their own meaningful experiences – either to enjoy alone, or to share with others. The focus is on people and on time in the context of the experience.

A Philips Design study on experience design

An example of a possible application issued from the experience design approach is the concept Nebula, presented at the Milan Furniture Fair in April 2001.

Nebula is an interactive projection system designed to enrich the experience of going to bed, sleeping and waking up. It provides an intuitive and natural way of physically participating in a virtual experience, through simple body movements and gestures.

It aims at creating an atmosphere in the bedroom that encourages and enhances rest, reflection, conversation, intimacy, imagination and play. Nebula consists of a ceiling projector linked via the internet to a database of content. Once users have selected the content for projection, they can manipulate it simply by adjusting their sleeping positions and interacting with their partner while in bed. For example one algorithm in the system translates body positions and movements into moving imagery and text. Since the dynamics between individuals are random and unpredictable, the flow of content created by the couple will be unique and specific to them. In general, the ceiling projection becomes livelier as the participants become more active.

Content is selected by placing a smart 'pebble' into the bedside pocket. Each pebble corresponds to a different topic or theme. For example a 'cloud' pebble produces content related to clouds and the sky, while a 'poem' pebble produces content related to poetry and rhymes. The content also changes according to the time of day and the season. For example a cloud pebble will trigger a dark sky when viewed at night, but produces a bright, blue sky during the day.

Once the alarm clock is set, the system projects two dots onto opposite sides of the ceiling. During the night, the distance between the dots diminishes, visually illustrating the time remaining before the alarm goes off and making it possible to gauge the remaining sleeping time from the distance that is left between the two. When the dots collide, sound and images are combined to create an appropriate waking experience.

The system also allows users to incorporate their own messages and drawings into the projections. Simply write a note or sketch something on a piece of paper and place it underneath the alarm clock. When the alarm goes off, a snapshot of the note or illustration will be projected.

Pebbles can also contain games, such as ping-pong, which will only be revealed when a particular combination of sleeping positions has been assumed. Once the positions have been discovered and the game is revealed, the couple can activate the game at any time by holding the top section of the duvet cover. Pulling the duvet to the left or right controls the left and right movements in the game. Activating and playing the game requires the cooperation of two people working together.

Conclusion

Going back now to our original question of finding the new attractive qualities for the future market, at Philips design we believe that this cannot be achieved through a technology push. We believe that technology is one of the main pillars to stimulate innovation but not the only one.

On the other hand, design (as styling) is also not the answer but just an ephemeral way of embellishing products and services to please an increasingly demanding public.

We believe that the cutting edge in the technology arena will be obtained only if people are firmly put at the centre of research processes. This does not mean to go and ask people what they want for the future (they would not know!), but to deeply understand the socio-cultural arena in order to be able to provide engineers, scientists, designers and marketers with tools to create solutions that can answer people's emerging needs and desires.

We believe that high design, with its human-focused, multidisciplinary and research-based approach is the tool that will help us to provide our clients with relevant and meaningful solutions for the future.

(Source: Philips Design, 2002)

Discussion

User-centred design as part of a sustainability policy

There is a tension between the development of products that are designed simply for entertainment or amusement, and the need to consider the future well-being of the planet. All products use resources, and the more products that are developed, the greater the amount of resources that will be denied to future generations. As if that were not bad enough, the use of energy and toxic materials is changing the climate of the planet and causing health problems. You will be considering such issues in greater depth in later blocks.

However the user-centred approach described in the article does not necessarily lead to the development of goods purely for selfish pleasure. The example of the 'nebula' projector, which you read about in the article above, may seem quite trivial as an idea. You may simply want to go to bed to sleep rather than play ping-pong with the covers. However the concepts and technologies that were developed in this project are now being put to a more serious use.

Philips Electronics is a leading manufacturer of MRI scanners, as well as consumer products, and it has used the concept of ambient experience in its medical work (Figure 40). Undergoing a scan can be a daunting experience because it involves passing through the machine itself while lying absolutely still. A projection system like nebula is now being used to create calming environments within the scanner and includes such devices as fish or other figures that will hold their breath when the child needs to do so – a necessary step in some scanning procedures.

Understanding how people relate to products can help designers to combine products in new ways to minimise resource and energy use. It can also lead to the creation of products that not only endure but also give the user the feeling that value has been added.

The designers at Philips Design also have to work within the sustainability policy that Philips has developed, and this leads to good practice within the current boundaries. However, as you will see as you study this course further, even the good practice of the best companies may not be enough to avoid large-scale environmental problems in the long term.

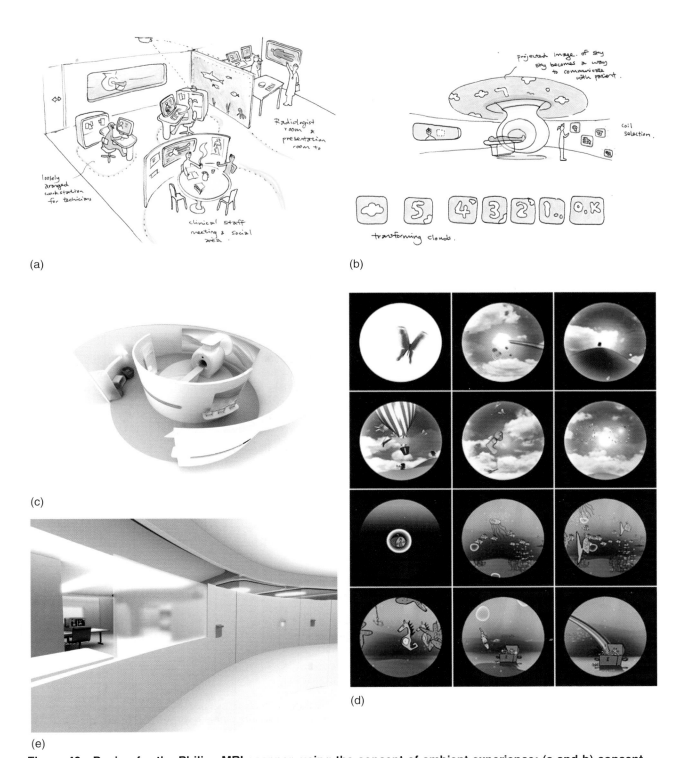

Figure 40   Design for the Philips MRI scanner, using the concept of ambient experience: (a and b) concept drawings; (c) model of scanner suite; (d) projected animation; (e) actual installed suite Source: Philips Electronics UK Ltd

SAQ 22

How has the focus of design evolved over the past 100 years?

SAQ 23

How have companies sought to expand markets?

SAQ 24

What is experience design?

5.5 User experience information on the DVDs

If you are near to your computer, this would be a good time to look at the T307 DVD videos 'Philips: designing for people' and 'Testing house'. You can also find more information about some of the methods used at Philips Design in the 'Philips: revisited' section on the T211 DVD.

The videos show several different ways user needs and experience are considered in the product development process. The videos also show methods used to gather and use information – methods include personas, feedback, stimulation and product testing.

Personas. Designers use information about users to create personas that bring information about user wants and needs to the product development process. (T211 DVD)

Feedback. Designers working directly with users gain feedback, and refine and develop product ideas and improvements. ('Designing for people' on T211 DVD)

Stimulation. Designers working directly with users are stimulated to come up with ideas for future product development. ('Designing for people' on T211 DVD)

Product testing. Testing houses gather information about users' experience of products at a late stage of the product development process to identify potential problems that may affect product success. And testing houses assess the user experience of products that are already on the market, to help consumers make informed purchasing decisions and to give feedback to companies. ('Testing house' on T307 DVD)

Key points of Section 5

- Design teams now include social scientists who can help designers to develop an empathic understanding of the users they are designing for.

- Observing people in their own contexts and environment or in a purpose-built observation laboratory can help to identify problems and stimulate ideas for solutions.

- Detailed questioning is a useful method for developing an understanding of how and why people relate to products.

- Although user research involves smaller numbers of people than conventional market research, it can lead to detailed and often unexpected insights, which stimulate innovative product ideas.

- Cultural probe techniques are helpful ways of engaging the interest and cooperation of potential users.

- Inclusive design, which addresses the needs of disabled users, frequently has benefits for able-bodied users as well.

- Testing houses are used both for formal performance testing and for user testing at all stages of product development.

- The usability of a product depends upon whether users can perceive the opportunities afforded by a product or understand the conventions used to interact with it.

6 Products and their markets

6.1 Selling the product

When a product has been fully designed and developed into a new product, the next, and most crucial, step is the launch of that product onto the marketplace. A number of critical decisions have to be made at this point to achieve a balance of the elements of the marketing mix (the 4 Ps and the new Ps). The right balance of elements can help to facilitate the rapid uptake of the new product by the target markets. For a radical innovation the factor of promotion may be critical in establishing both the value and the desirability of the new product. For an incremental innovation, the price factor may be of greater significance.

Sometimes companies choose to launch a product in a particular geographical area before launching it on a wider scale. This can be a way of testing the market before a national or international launch. It can also be used to evaluate the effectiveness of promotional campaigns if the product is put on sale in two areas simultaneously – in one area with promotional activity and in the other without.

One of the most important aspects of the physical placing of a product is to get the product to the customer when it is required. This demands an efficient distribution system based on accurate forecasts of sales figures. The information gathered by the market decision support system is used to inform these predictions and plan both the production and distribution of the product.

In Section 2 I discussed how potential markets are opened up when potential customers have sufficient interest, money and access to a product. For the company selling a new product the task, once the product has been created, is to drum up sufficient interest through promotional strategies and to ensure access by developing efficient distribution systems to ensure the product can reach potential markets when purchasers want it.

But care is needed. If a company has promoted the imminent launch of a new product heavily, and then fails to meet its own deadlines, this can lead to loss of sales that undermines the success of a product. Similar problems can arise if a product is launched to meet a self-promoted deadline when there are still technical difficulties. This situation can lead to the product developing a reputation for being unreliable, which adversely affects future sales.

The destinations of manufacturers' products are diverse and depend upon the product and its targeted market. Consumer products may be destined for specialist shops, small general shops, department stores, DIY stores, super-retailers and even shops in garages, whereas commercial and industrial products may be going to wholesalers, agents or direct to purchasers.

6.1.1 Direct marketing and mass customisation

In general the more complex the range of products offered by a company, the less likely it is to sell directly to the customer. However some companies choose to market their products directly to the final purchaser through the internet, mail-order selling, doorstep sales or company-owned stores. One benefit of this system to the manufacturer is that it can know immediately how many products are required and can adjust production accordingly. However direct marketing does mean the company has to invest more in order processing and distribution than it would if those functions were being performed by a wholesaler.

Doorstep selling has declined with the growth of retailers but is still used in some industries, and there are variations on this form of direct selling. An example of this type of selling is product parties, whereby agents demonstrate a company's products at a gathering of friends and the host receives a small amount of commission, a 'gift', for any sales made. One company that is well known for employing this strategy is Tupperware, which makes plastic containers and other items for use in the kitchen.

One of the most prevalent forms of direct marketing now is the use of the internet. This is widely used for the sale of all sorts of goods and has enabled some small companies to reach a worldwide market. However, as I discussed earlier, large companies such as car manufacturers are now using this medium as a way to take orders from customers and inform customers about their products.

6.1.2 Sales promotion

Different promotional strategies are appropriate at different stages of the product's life. A radically new product needs to be launched onto the market in a way that helps potential purchasers to understand what the product does, as well as selling the idea that it is worth buying.

This can be achieved in various ways, depending on the product and the market. New products that might be expected to have widespread consumer sales can be advertised through a combination of media: newspaper and magazine advertising, posters, radio, television, email and the internet. Advertising campaigns can also be supported by in-store displays and leaflets. Products with a more limited market might be advertised on the internet or in specialist magazines and journals, but can also be supported by in-store displays and information, where appropriate.

One approach to sales promotion is to offer wholesalers and retailers incentives to stock and promote a company's products. Incentives may include offering more profit on particular products, giving allowances for advertising, discounts for quantity, and paying for in-store promotions and displays to assist the selling of the product. These are known as *push* strategies. The other approach is to encourage the consumer to seek out the product, using promotional campaigns such as coupons and money-off offers. These are known as *pull* strategies.

6.2 Product–service relationship

As technology develops, the boundaries between products and services become more blurred. Take for example the Apple iPod. The iPod was launched as a portable music player onto which owners can download their favourite CD tracks from their home computers. The original iPod was able to hold 1000 music tracks – enough for an extensive music collection.

However the product was extended by the opening of the Apple iTunes site. This site enables people to purchase tracks, or even whole albums, and download them onto their computers. The software enables users to create play lists and compilations that can be put onto the iPod and stored and manipulated there.

In its first year of trading in the USA the Apple iTunes store sold over 70 million music tracks at a cost of 99 US cents each. When launched in Europe Apple iTunes sold 800 000 tunes in the first week of trading, at a cost per track of €0.99 (about £0.80). There are now lots of similar sites offering a similar service for other music players, but the music format used on the iPod requires the user to purchase music exclusively from the Apple iTunes store. The launch of the video iPod in 2005 led to the iTunes store offering video as well as music.

Another strong example of the product–service relationship is the range of facilities offered by mobile phone companies in addition to the straightforward use of the phone for telephoning or text messaging – for example information about sporting events sent to your phone, downloadable ring tones, pictures and web browser services.

While the relationship between product and service may be clear in some consumer electronics industries such as music and computing, similar relationships can be seen emerging in more unexpected areas. For example manufacturers of white goods have been exploring internet-connected appliances such as microwaves, washing machines and fridges. For fridges and microwaves, the research has been into making intelligent appliances that can sense what food has been used and build a shopping list that can be sent direct to the supermarket for doorstep delivery. For washing machines research is looking at making machines updatable, for example sending a new set of instructions to the machine's electronic interface to offer improved wash performance through new wash programmes.

Even in the non-electronic industries, service elements have become more important in the sale of goods. As you saw earlier in the discussion of the marketing mix, aftersales service may be an important element when choosing between similar products.

6.2.1 Total product concept

The interplay between product function, added features or services and the pre- and post-purchase experience can be summarised as the concept of the *total product*. Products can be viewed at three levels (Figure 41). These levels are identified as:

1   core product

2   actual product

3   total product.

Figure 41 Total product concept Source: adapted from Levitt (1986)

To show what this means in practice I will take the digital camera as an example.

The *core* product includes the functions the product offers, for example a camera that takes photographs and short videos and saves them in a digital format.

The *actual* product includes all the aspects that affect purchasers' perceptions of the product itself, such as quality, styling, features, packaging and branding. Information about reliability and ease of use, where known, may also form part of the perceptions of the product. For example a camera may be made by a company associated with photography that has received good reviews in consumer association and photography magazines. It may also come packaged with software to enable the manipulation of photographs on a computer and a trial subscription to an online image storage bank.

The *total* product includes aspects external to the product itself that may influence the purchasing decision, for example delivery, installation, servicing and warranties. For a camera this may include tutorials on the manufacturer's website, a technical helpdesk to troubleshoot problems and assist those having problems setting up the camera and software, and aftersales service for repairs and maintenance.

The concept of the total product is applicable to products in all market sectors. In any market, the purchaser will be looking for key product features and seeking assurance of quality and reliability. However, when choosing between similar products, factors such as possible delivery times, installation and maintenance may strongly affect which of the competing products is purchased.

The contention is that products compete on factors at the actual and total product level, and therefore their perceived value can be increased by paying attention to these factors as much as to the product itself.

If you look back to the article on 'The evolving roles of technology and design' in the previous section, you can see how the developments in design can be mapped onto this model. The core product is concerned with function and performance, the actual product with value-added features, and the total product with the design of the whole user experience.

Some commentators argue that future economic growth will be based not simply on goods and services but on a range of experiences and transformations that may involve both of these elements.

The term experience design is used in more than one way. Product designers talk about experience design with specific reference to a product or group of products. However the term can also be used to describe the design of shopping environments, theme parks, restaurants and even internet sites – indeed any place where people come to spend time and money.

In many ways the design of experience, whether it is of a product, a real space or a virtual space, has similar elements. The product or place needs to function properly and to encourage repeat purchases or return visits, and the design should delight and make users feel good about their choice.

Of course the ways this is achieved for products and places is different. For a product the delight factor may be an aesthetic quality that delights the eye and textures that please the sense of touch. For a place the delight may come from the whole sensory experience of the environment or it may come from extras such as free treats, for example giving balloons or goodie bags to children.

Beyond experience design there is the design for *transformation*. A company that is in the business of transformation will be charging not for goods or services but for a demonstrable outcome achieved by the customer. Such businesses can readily be seen in the areas of medicine, for example laser eye surgery to correct sight problems, cosmetic surgery and osteopathy.

However businesses or organisations that develop skills might also be said to be in the transformation business, whether these are sports skills or the cognitive skills developed through education and training.

SAQ 25

What is the total product concept?

SAQ 26

What factors influence perceptions of the actual (or formal) product?

SAQ 27

Name three factors that may influence the total (or augmented) product.

6.3 Designing product ranges

The products of large manufacturing companies are rarely designed in isolation. More often designers are called upon to design a range of products that have the same basic purpose but that differ in the features they offer. You will be familiar with a wide range of consumer products and cars, and similar ranges exist in all market sectors. For the manufacturer, managing the product range presents a number of challenges.

An overview of the performance of the entire product range in terms of sales and costs is needed to inform future product development. For example it may be noted that a particular product is selling well while the sales of a cheaper version are less buoyant. This may indicate that customers are prepared to pay more for the value-added features of the more expensive model because it offers greater advantages. Using research to understand this purchasing behaviour may lead to a revised product range.

Within most companies' product portfolios it is usually possible to identify different products that are selling at different rates and making different levels of profit. The Boston Consulting Group created the matrix in Figure 42 to describe the sales performance of different products.

	High market share	Low market share
High market growth	 star	 problem child
Low market growth	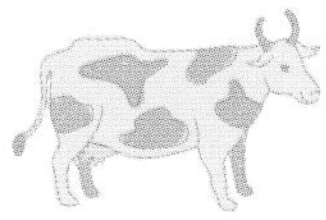 cash cow	 dog
Negative market growth	 war horse	 dodo

Figure 42   Matrix identifying different categories of product by their growth and market share

6.3.1 Stars

These products diffuse rapidly and dominate the market. Often the costs of maintaining growth are high but these costs are seen as necessary to establish a position as market leader. Eventually, as they move through the natural product life cycle, all stars decline. An example of a star is the Apple iPod, which in 2003–2004 dominated the personal player market but had to defend its position in the face of a lot of competition.

6.3.2 Cash cows

These are former stars that have achieved market dominance but are in a mature phase of their life cycle so have low market growth. These products are generating much of a company's profits and may be financing the stars. There are many examples in the food industry, such as cereals, fizzy drinks and chocolate bars.

6.3.3 Dogs

These are products with low market share and low market growth. Although these products will be generating some profit, the decision to be made is whether the production plant could be used to make something more profitable.

6.3.4 Problem child

This is the name given to products that have a small share of a growing market. The challenge for the company is to find a way to increase the market share and turn a problem child into a star.

6.3.5 War horses

These are products that have a high share of a market that is declining. The decision to be made is whether the product can be revived or whether the decline is irreversible. Sometimes it is possible to revive interest in such a product by aiming at a new market.

6.3.6 Dodos

These are products with a low market share in a declining market, and commercially it makes sense to discontinue them.

Companies use the information gathered from their marketing decision support system to make decisions about which products to improve, which products to carry out further market research on, which products to promote and which products to discontinue, alongside decisions about possible areas for new product development.

The skill of business lies in finding a balance between the different product groups. Although, at first sight, it may seem that a company should focus of all its money and attention on cash cows, other product categories may have an important role in forming the image of the company brand as a whole. For example a car manufacturer may have a high-cost problem child product that attracts attention and brings customers in to buy a lower-price cash cow product.

The role of design in the creation of a product portfolio is crucial. Well-designed products that address user needs and give products an edge over the competition are more likely to end up as stars and cash cows than poorly designed products that compete only on price.

6.3.7 Product positioning

When new products are launched onto the market, their position, relative to other products, has to be established so that potential purchasers can perceive their advantages and relevance to their own needs and wants. This *product positioning* is achieved through promotional strategies such as advertising, in-store displays and write-ups in newspapers and magazines.

Market research techniques, as discussed earlier in this block, are used to monitor the position of the product and how the product is perceived, both before and after any advertising campaign. In cases where a user-centred approach to design has been adopted, the positioning of a new product may have been considered throughout the development process, and the marketing strategies used may reflect this, for example advertising the fact the product has been developed in conjunction with users.

6.3.8 Marketing strategies

The case below gives some insight into the marketing activities used to launch an innovative product onto the market. Although the example given concerns US markets, you will recognise that identical strategies are used all over the world.

Case study **Selling hybrid cars**

Toyota launched its first version of a hybrid petrol–electric car, the Toyota Prius, in 1997 (Figure 43). The car was sold first in Japan and then worldwide. In 1999 Toyota offered five US families, in 12 cities, a chance to test-drive the Prius for a month. There were over 15 000 applications to do this. This research was carried out to see how well the Prius was adapted to the US market and lifestyles.

Figure 43 Toyota Prius hybrid car Source: Toyota Manufacturing (UK) Ltd

In 2003, when the second generation of the Prius was launched, Toyota decided to try to increase its share of the US market. Toyota's nearest competitor in this market was Honda, which also makes a hybrid vehicle. The launch of the car was assisted by US government tax incentives for clean-fuel vehicles – this deducted $2000 off any car bought before the end of 2003. The total purchase price was around $20 000.

The launch of the new Prius was accompanied by a high-profile, multifaceted, product-specific advertising and marketing campaign. Toyota adopted the interesting strategy of using two different advertising agencies simultaneously, reflecting the hybrid nature of the car. In the first half of 2003 $12 million was spent on advertising – half of this amount was spent on television commercials.

The Saatchi and Saatchi advertising campaign had the slogan, 'The power to move forward', and it focused on the innovative technology of the hybrid synergy drive, its low emissions and its fuel efficiency. Sixteen television advertisements were created and shown on a variety of different television channels. Saatchi and Saatchi also developed some non techno-centric advertisements, which emphasised the environmental benefits of the car with slogans such as, 'One small step on the accelerator, one giant leap for mankind' and 'It's been a long time since transportation truly advanced but now we have good news for planet Earth'.

Follow-up market research conducted in Detroit showed that 62 per cent of people interviewed had little knowledge of the nature of hybrid cars, 10 per cent of respondents had not heard of hybrid cars, a further 28 per cent thought that hybrid cars may have to be plugged in to be charged up, and 24 per cent were convinced that plugging in was necessary for recharging. In response to this research, two more commercials were created, which ended on the slogan, 'Low emissions, high mileage and you never have to plug it in'.

In addition to television advertising, Toyota used printed advertisements in newspapers and magazines and also outdoor advertising posters, all of which emphasised the environmental benefits of the car. Another promotional strategy used was to offer a Prius as a prize in a draw, with the ticket sales having the dual purpose of gathering information on potential customers. Celebrity endorsement was also used to raise the profile of the car, using actors such as Cameron Diaz and Bill Maher.

The Toyota website was also developed so that it contained a micro-site for the Prius where information on the car and dealerships could be found alongside the interactivity to customise and obtain pricing information about the car. Existing Prius owners were mailed with an invitation to buy the new car ahead of its launch to the public. A total of 18 000 'Prius pioneers' were emailed with a similar invitation. The internet was also used to mail electronic newsletters addressed to Prius owners and enthusiasts. The newsletters included information about government incentive schemes as well as owners' stories.

As well as the promotional activity around the Prius itself, Toyota was promoting its brand image through general advertising, putting forward a view of an innovative, environmentally aware company. The corporation used market research to develop an understanding of consumer attitudes towards the brand while using strategies such as involvement in charity activities to raise the company profile, particularly among certain groups, such as the US Hispanic communities.

The combined results of these promotional activities in 2003 was to increase the sales of cars from 12 000 in 2000 to more than 50 000. Production, which was originally planned for 6000 units per month, was increased to 10 000 units per month to meet demand. In 2004 the production plan was to make 47 000 Prius cars, which was a 31 per cent increase on Toyota's original planning figures. In February 2005 Toyota announced plans to double its production capacity in the USA to 100 000 cars each year because would-be purchasers in some parts of the USA were waiting for several months to buy a Prius.

Toyota's target markets for the Prius fell into three types of buyer: the techno-savvy who likes to own the latest technology, the environmentally conscious and the value conscious. In 2003 a typical Prius buyer was a middle-aged female (average age 53) with an average income of $87 000. Moreover 82 per cent of buyers were college educated and 67 per cent were married.

This is an interesting contrast to the buyer profile for the competing Honda Hybrid cars. A typical Honda buyer in 2003 was a professional man, in his mid-40s, with an annual income of $55 000 dollars, buying the car as the family's second or third vehicle.

Exercise 18   Driving home the message

What are the challenges for a company promoting an environmentally friendly product? What aspects of the product did Toyota's advertising emphasise and how effective was this?

Discussion

The Toyota case is interesting because it shows the many-stranded approach the company felt necessary to adopt to compete in the US market, where there is a history of using fuel-heavy vehicles. The challenge is to try to persuade potential purchasers that an environmentally friendly product, in this case a fuel-efficient car, has sufficient advantages over the product they are familiar with.

The advertising campaigns emphasised two things – technical innovation and environmental benefits. The campaigns appear to have been reasonably successful, particularly with environmentally conscious women. However the buyer profile suggests that perhaps the campaigns have been less successful at attracting the techno-savvy group. This may be because Toyota's competitors, Honda, had already established its brand with this market group.

Key points of Section 6

- When a product has been developed and produced it needs to be sold. Consumer products are sold in a variety of ways, including over the internet.

- The boundaries between products and services are blurring, and the service elements are important in the competition between competing products.

- Products can be thought of on a number of levels – the core product, the actual product and the total product.

- Products sell at different rates and have differing shares of the market. Looking at product ranges in terms of market share and market growth can help companies to identify products to support or discontinue.

- Understanding how a product is perceived by markets can help companies to develop advertising and sales strategies to shift perceptions and appeal to the preferences of the target market.

7 Markets, cultures and design

7.1 Cultural contexts

In this block you have already seen how market research techniques, user-centred design and design for the environment are being used within companies to gain a competitive edge. To help them in this work, designers need to understand the context of the users – not just their physical context but also their psychological, social and cultural context.

Almost 300 years ago, Jonathan Swift wrote in his satire *Gulliver's Travels* about the people of the imaginary land of Balnibarbi, who had taken up the suggestions of the scientists there to communicate using things rather than words.

> Since words are only names for things it would be more convenient for all men to carry about them such things as were necessary to express the particular business they are to discourse on ... I have often beheld two of those sages almost sinking under the weight of their packs, like pedlars among us; who, when they met in the streets, would lay down their loads, open their sacks, and hold conversation for an hour together; then put up their implements, help each other to resume their burthens, and take their leave.

> But for short conversations, a man may carry implements in his pockets and under his arms, enough to supply him, and in his house he cannot be at a loss; therefore the room where company meet is full of all things ready at hand, requisite to furnish mater for this kind of artificial converse.

(Swift, 1994)

It would seem fair to assume that in the eighteenth century, people's attachment to objects was as strong as it is in the twenty-first century. This extract probably has even wider resonance today than it did in Swift's time. Picture young people in the street, comparing mobile phones or music players and carrying out an almost wordless conversation about their features.

In the wealthiest nations of the world, widespread ownership of things is taken for granted, and manufacturers compete to sell consumers the things they make. But the story does not end there. The products that are bought become part of the culture of their purchasers, expressing and reinforcing values, beliefs and attitudes.

The social sciences are now frequently drawn upon to inform, explain and research consumer preferences. The discipline of psychology assists in the understanding of perceptions and motivations, while anthropology and ethnography assist in the understanding of group behaviour and cultural preferences. The brief explanations that follow show some of the ways these bodies of knowledge can bring insights to the market research and design process by helping researchers and designers to ask the right questions.

7.2 Psychology and markets

Psychology, the study of mind and behaviour, offers an understanding of why people buy products.

Broadly speaking there are two schools of thought about how people learn about the world – connectionist theories and cognitive theories.

7.2.1 Connectionist theories

Connectionist theories see people as developing particular behaviours in response to stimuli. The success of some advertising campaigns and the habitual buying behaviour of consumers can be explained, to some extent, by some of these theories.

For example often-repeated advertising jingles may stimulate purchasers to buy the product when they spot it in a shop. Likewise purchasers may routinely purchase certain products when shopping, without giving any thought for the alternatives, because this is an established habit.

Retailers use stimuli to provoke a response from buyers. For example the smell of fresh bread in supermarkets is deliberately created to stimulate the purchase of bread and related foods.

However the value of connectionist theories is limited when trying to understand the perceptions and motivations of potential purchasers. For this, the theories of cognitive psychologists are more appropriate.

7.2.2 Cognitive theories

Cognitive theories view people as learning about the world through their knowledge, perception and experience of it, and gaining new insights through the solving of problems.

Attitudes towards products are affected by what people *know* about those products and what they *believe* about them. A purchaser may know from their previous experience of a product that it meets their needs but they may also hold certain beliefs about that product, for example it is not good value for money. In addition perceptions will be affected by both the attitude and the disposition of the purchaser – someone who is concerned about the environment may be prepared to take extra effort to purchase a product that is ecofriendly.

Perceptions

In the discussion on the design of product ranges, you saw how market research may include perceptual mapping to understand how products are viewed in relation to each other.

Perceptions of products are affected by all of the senses – sight, feel, sound, smell, taste – as well as intuition. Designers who are aware of this will seek to design products that satisfy all of the senses. For example in the design of cars, as well as the aesthetic styling, factors such as the sound made by the doors closing, the feel of the steering wheel and even the smell of the upholstery are all considered important to creating a car that will meet the expectations and hopes of potential purchasers.

One of the theories of cognitive psychology is known as gestalt (German for 'configurations'). This theory describes how an object is seen as more than the sum of its individual parts. In other words all of the perceptions of different aspects of a product, and beliefs, knowledge and previous experience are brought together in the viewer's mind to give an overall perception of that product.

Occasionally designers create a product that attains a cult status that cannot be explained simply by looking at the component parts. The original Volkswagen (VW) of the mid-1930s was such a successful design that designers actively sought to reproduce this gestalt in the new VW Beetle, introduced in the 1990s (Figure 44).

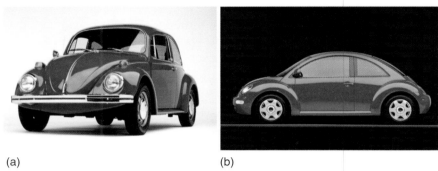

(a)　　　　　　　　　　　　　　　　　(b)

Figure 44　(a) Original VW Beetle of the 1930s. (b) VW Beetle of the 1990s.
Source: Volkswagen UK

For marketers, research based on cognitive theories will explore consumer knowledge, perceptions and experience. Marketing campaigns will be designed to appeal to the senses and, where needed, offer information to assist the potential purchaser to understand the product. For designers the challenge is to bring together any insights into users' and purchasers' perceptions, and to embody these in a new product.

For radical innovations the challenges are greater. Potential purchasers may have little or no knowledge of the product. Everett Rogers (2003) says there are five criteria for the successful diffusion of products. Of these, *relative advantage* (offering a competitive advantage) over existing products, *complexity* (being easy to use) and *compatibility* (matching existing products) are all directly concerned with potential purchasers' perceptions of the product. *Observability* (seeing the product in use) and *trialability* (trying the product out) are concerned with purchasers coming close enough to the product to develop favourable perceptions of it.

Radical innovations may require information and knowledge development, as well as an appeal to the senses. Similar challenges are presented by sustainable alternatives to existing products.

Persuading purchasers to switch from established products or ways of doing things to unknown and untried products and methods demands a shift in both perceptions and behaviour. When the Apple G4 iMac computer was launched, a multipage advertising booklet was inserted into newspapers. Apple's Switch advertising campaign focused on dispelling myths about Macintosh computers and their compatibility with other personal computers. As part of the campaign a website (Figure 45) told the stories of 'real' people from different backgrounds who had switched from a personal computer to a Macintosh computer.

Figure 45 Apple Switch campaign Source: Apple Computer

In terms of the total product concept, not only do the core benefits of the product have to be seen to have advantages but the messages given out by styling, packaging and so on have to be strong enough to encourage purchases. In addition, for complex products, the support systems that are in place to get the new product up and running need to be easy to use and efficient.

The driving force taking people from a perception of needs to an action such as buying a product is known as *motivation*. Everyone has motives, which are the inner drivers that make people act to attain goals.

When a need is perceived a tension is created that is released only when that need is satisfied, a more urgent need has supplanted it or something more compelling has grabbed the person's attention. For example in well-fed affluent countries, when a person is hungry they have a strong motivation to eat, but they can sometimes be distracted from this by the desire to finish what they are doing or by a more interesting opportunity that presents itself. In a country where there is famine or war, motivations and distractions may be different.

Psychologists have created many different ways of classifying motives in their efforts to understand this complex area better. Some of these classifications are:

- *Biogenic* or *psychogenic*. Biogenic motives are biological, for example hunger, thirst, safety. Psychogenic motives are psychological, for example social, cultural, emotional and intellectual needs.

- *Learned* or *unlearned*. Learned motives are those that are acquired through the individual's interaction with the world. Unlearned motives are instinctive.

- *Rational* or *emotional*. Rational motives are based on logical thinking. Emotional motives are based on feeling.

- *Conscious* or *unconscious*. Conscious motives are those motives that the individual is aware of. Unconscious motives are deep-seated motives that the individual is not aware of.

Often motivation is complex. For example a purchaser may approach a purchasing decision with a number of different motives. The purchase of a new car may be motivated by the conscious, rational motivation to find a car that is reliable and comes out well in consumer tests. However the purchaser may also have a strong but unconscious emotional motivation to buy a car that will make him or her feel powerful.

An understanding of motivation in both the design and marketing process can help to create products that appeal to potential customers on a number of different levels, in that they perform and function well, appeal to the conscious, rational motives of the purchaser, and are endowed with aesthetic qualities that appeal to potential purchasers' unconscious, emotional motives. This applies in all market sectors – while function, performance and price may appeal to the rational motives of the industrial or public sector buyer, aesthetic qualities that appeal to different motives may help a purchaser to decide between competing products, as you can see in this extract:

> Successful industrial product manufacturers know the sales value of attractive design, as the following example illustrates. A Canadian pump manufacturer approached consultant designers to redesign its range of pumps. Some ... business colleagues were asked why it was thought necessary to have their machines redesigned, because, after all, these only go underground. 'Maybe', the pump manufacturer replied, 'but they are not bought underground.'

(Chisnall, 1994)

7.3   Cultures and markets

Ethnographers and anthropologists study people within groups and their cultures. There is debate among social scientists about the precise definition of the word culture but, broadly speaking, the study of culture concerns behaviours that are shared and transmitted by members of particular groups in society. These behaviours are 'learned' from other members of the group.

The key idea is that attitudes, values and beliefs are shared by members of a group, and these are transmitted to other members of the group, thereby affecting their behaviour. The cultural orientation of a group – or the culture a group adopts – can be affected by many variables, for example nationality, age, sex, social group, education, profession, ethnicity and religion.

As well as a shared view of the world around them, cultural groups also have their own cultural norms. Cultural norms are standards of behaviour that have become established as the way to act in given situations. These can be divided into folkways and mores. *Folkways* are social conventions such as dressing for dinner or sending Christmas cards. *Mores* (pronounced morays) are norms that are central to the cultural group, such as religious or moral beliefs associated with family life and national identity.

Cultural norms affect the decisions and actions that individuals take every day, including their purchasing behaviour. Indeed for many people, ownership of products is a way of identifying and belonging to a cultural group. Culture offers people a sense of identity and social cohesion, which may profoundly affect their purchasing behaviour. Products are seen as vehicles of cultural meanings – in other words products have a symbolic as well as a functional role. Purchasers choose and use these cultural meanings to express themselves.

Anthropologists, working with designers, will research the symbolic significance and cultural meaning of products and feed their understanding into the product development process so that the product, its packaging and the associated sales campaign will appeal to identified cultural groups. They will also carry out research to determine the effectiveness of promotional campaigns and track the effects of the product and promotional campaign on perceptions, attitudes and buying behaviours.

Cultural groups may be as large as a nation or group of nations, or as small as a handful of people. Designers may be interested in cultures of any size. For example it is important to understand national cultures to design products that will be widely acceptable. Different nations may view products completely differently, as you saw with the earlier example of vacuum cleaners designed by Philips for the European and Asian markets.

At the other end of the scale studying the culture of small subgroups, as manifested in their lifestyles, can lead to new ideas for products that, ultimately, may have a wider appeal. Some large manufacturers, particularly in the fashion industry, employ researchers to 'culture watch'. The researchers try to spot emerging trends among small trendsetting groups that can be translated into mass-market products. For example Nike observed the youth subcultures seen on London streets and used these to stimulate ideas for a new trainer shoe that would be seen as cool (desirable) to young people.

Creating innovative products poses an interesting challenge for designers. The design team requires an understanding of cultural groups and their attitudes, values and beliefs, including their relationships with products. The designers' challenge is to embody these values and beliefs into an object.

When the designers are designing for a cultural group with which they identify, the task is significantly easier than designing for a group that holds completely different values. The value of user-centred research and design is in creating empathy between the design team and the cultural groups, with whom they may have little or nothing in common.

7.4 Markets and organisations

The discussions above have centred largely on finding out about the consumer product market. However many purchases are made on behalf of companies rather than individuals. Some products that are bought on behalf of companies are similar to those bought by the consumer sector but the purchasing process is usually different. Other products, bought for the industrial, commercial and public sectors, are completely different from consumer goods – for example high-cost capital equipment or a production plant bought as large, one-off purchases, or products that will be used as components by the purchasing company.

Purchasers within organisations have to deal with the demands of that organisation while managing their relationships with suppliers. As is the case with purchasers in the consumer market, they will have their personal perceptions and motivations, which will inevitably affect their decision-making.

Buying for organisations frequently entails negotiation, and these negotiations may be as coloured by cultural behaviours as any consumer purchase, particularly when the negotiators are from different national groups and have differing expectations of behaviour. To avoid misunderstandings and help the negotiations to succeed, understanding is needed. For example Japanese business protocol and etiquette is somewhat different to that of the UK. Reflective silences are acceptable in a Japanese meeting but may be seen as indicative of a problem in a meeting in the UK.

7.4.1 Categories of industrial products

Industrial products can be classified into five categories based on the nature of those products.

- Raw materials

    These are materials that have not been processed, for example mineral ores, timber or raw foodstuffs.

- Fabricating materials and parts

    These are partly processed components. Fabricating materials will be processed by the purchasing company, for example wool, which will be woven into a textile. Fabricating parts will be bought in and used without change, for example screws, plugs and other components. In a public sector organisation, such as a hospital, examples might be resin casts for setting broken bones, or pharmaceuticals.

- Installations

    These are large industrial products that determine the capabilities and scale of the purchasing organisation and that are most frequently made to order, for example production plant, aircraft or ships. For the public sector hospital an installation might be an item such as an MRI scanner. In the commercial sector an installation could be a complex computer system. Installations are usually very expensive items and are expected to have a long life.

- Accessory equipment

  This is equipment that is necessary for the operation of a company but that does not have a direct bearing on the finished product. Examples in all sectors might be personal computers and office equipment, power tools and vehicles.

- Operating supplies

  These are low-priced goods that are needed for an organisation to operate effectively but that are not part of the organisational products or outcome, for example stationery supplies, cleaning materials and fuel.

7.4.2 Risks and roles

A major concern for organisational purchasers is balancing profit and risk. For operating supplies the risks are small because costs are low. However for installations, purchasing decisions are high risk because of the costs involved and the importance of the purchase to the organisation's key business. Buying an automatic production plant is a major capital investment, and it is critical for the purchasing organisation that this equipment is delivered and installed on time, and runs without problem, to enable the company to make products that will repay this investment.

For the supplying company, meeting order deadlines and supplying products that meet the purchasers' demands is vital for repeat orders and for the company's reputation in the industry. Many suppliers find themselves in a position where they have one or two main customers, and in such a situation the supplying company's fortunes rest on the quality of their products and the relationship between the company and the purchaser(s).

Within an organisation different roles may be identified in the buying process. Although it is possible for one person to take on all of these roles, more frequently they are carried out by a number of different people. These roles are gatekeeper, influencer, decider, buyer and user.

Gatekeepers collect the information that will be used to identify potential suppliers. *Influencers* may exert a subtle influence on the buying decision. *Buyers* place the purchasing order, while *deciders* make the purchasing decision. *Users* are those who will be using the product, and although they may influence the purchaser in terms of what is required of the product, they will not make the commercial decision.

The implications for designers and marketers are that the product itself and the marketing strategies have to appeal at different levels to people with different motivations. Marketers have to be aware of the role of the person they are communicating to in order to pitch their marketing strategy at the right level.

7.5 Prevailing designs

The relationships between design and culture are complex and interlinked. Different products are adopted by different cultural groups because these products are seen to embody the cultural values of that group. Designers try to meet the needs and wishes of cultural groups but they are often doing this within the context of prevailing design trends.

Such trends can usually be spotted in products designed at around the same time. These are often, but not exclusively, aesthetic trends that are gradually transmitted from product to product, lending a visual cohesion to the age. For example it is possible to identify objects from previous ages or decades because they have a certain similarity of style and often use similar materials. In the 1930s Europe was looking forward to a new future. Many of the objects of that time embodied these aspirations and new materials such as bakelite and laminated plastic allowed for new shapes and finishes (Figure 46).

Figure 46　'Chapel' radio, 1938 Source: Philips Electronics

By the 1950s the UK was emerging from the economic hardship brought about by war and planning the new future. Many of the objects of that time were the result of new production technologies, and materials such as plastics and laminates created futuristic looking shapes and finishes.

Design styles reflect a number of things, including the zeitgeist (spirit of the age), prevalent or common technologies, and the prevailing culture of designers themselves.

In the early twenty-first century, references to previous eras of design styling are common and styles are diverse, but embedded microelectronics, touch control and displays are common in electrical products, and new generations of plastics are seen with similar finishes in many different types of products. The Emotive Micro audio systems launched by Philips in 2003 embodied the same technology with three different finishes to appeal to different cultural groups (Figure 47).

Figure 47 One of the Emotive Micro audio systems with a rugged, high-impact appearance Source: Philips

For most purchasers the designer of the products they are purchasing is unknown. Even so, consumers see designers' products in the media and, although the designer's name is not remembered, they may adjust their perceptions and expectations and seek out products that are design statements.

However there are some 'star' designers, who have made a name for themselves in product design in the same way as some haute couturiers are known for their innovative fashion collections. These design stars, although often designing for small markets, can exert a wider influence on design. The design profession views the products of star designers and assimilates these new designs into the palette of possibilities.

The original Apple iMac was designed by Jonathan Ive, who can be described as a star designer. The iMac led to stationery accessories whose style was attributable to the iMac's brightly coloured, translucent plastic (Figure 48). The iMac's plastic body style was copied for computer peripherals, then for desk accessories and later for a wide range of objects.

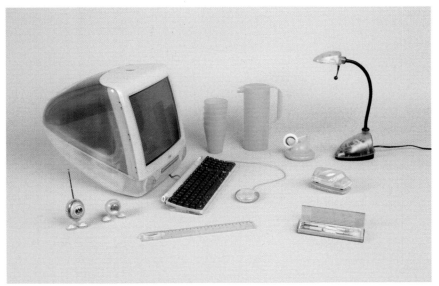

Figure 48 Original Apple iMac (left) and some examples of products whose style is attributable to the popularity of the iMac

SAQ 28

Why is it helpful for designers to know about perceptions and cultures?

SAQ 29

What influences purchasing decisions in an industrial setting?

Key points of Section 7

- Market research and user-centred design techniques are all ways of finding out about the cultures of potential purchasers. Understanding the psychology of potential users can help designers to ask the right questions and design products or promotional materials that are perceived as attractive.

- Radical innovations demand a perceptual shift from potential purchasers, which means the total product must have a strong appeal.

- Understanding what motivates people to buy products can help to design and sell them

- Studying cultural groups can stimulate ideas for design.

- Creating products for industrial and commercial markets also entails an understanding of perceptions, motivations and cultures at an organisational level, where there are a number of roles in the buying process.

- Each era has prevailing designs that share characteristics of aesthetics, materials use or technologies.

8 Global production and world markets

8.1 Internationalism and globalisation

In the latter half of the twentieth century many manufacturing companies shifted from a national to a global perspective when it came to selling and making products. Designing for worldwide markets brings its own challenges. To design and manage a wide range of products that meet the needs of different cultural groups can be costly. However if this is not done, the company may not be able to compete on the global market.

Marketers need to be aware of cultural differences when devising marketing campaigns and branding and packaging their products. A product name that has positive meanings in one culture may have negative meanings in another – for example General Motors' Vauxhall Nova car (taken from the Latin for 'new') caused amusement in Spain, where Nova means 'doesn't go'.

Global production allows manufacturers to take advantages of the most competitive component prices and labour costs worldwide. The cost of shipping is low when set against the savings from the manufacture of components or products in emerging countries. In the early twenty-first century many manufacturers shifted their manufacturing bases to China, where labour costs are significantly lower than in Europe.

For design teams the challenge of remote production is to communicate design ideas and discuss manufacturing implications across cultures. This is another reason for making some effort to understanding cultural differences. Some large manufacturers base design teams at their remote manufacturing facilities to facilitate clear communication.

Smaller companies that outsource the production of components or products to a remote manufacturer have to develop processes to check the manufacturer's understanding of the design and its specification. Failure to communicate can lead to a spectrum of problems, from minor problems of design detailing to major problems such as a product failing to meet safety standards or to perform adequately.

8.1.1 Global markets

Despite designers' best efforts, global sales of products are affected not only by the product's appeal to potential purchasers but also by political and economic factors affecting the diffusion of products worldwide, such as:

- Trade agreements and trade barriers

  There are a number of trade agreements in operation between different nations. An example is the European Union, which enables member states to trade virtually without customs duties. Trade barriers are usually economic measures to limit the import of goods, to give an advantage to home industries.

- Relationships between nations

  Disputes between governments can sometimes lead to trade embargoes, whereby one nation or group of nations refuses to trade with another – this happens particularly when those nations have been at war.

- Political instability and wars

  Wars and political instability can have a devastating effect on trade, preventing both imports and exports of goods.

- Incomes

  At the beginning of this block I discussed how, for a market to exist, potential purchasers must have the income to buy the product. Some nations have a low per capita income, but the distribution of wealth is such that there are significant numbers of wealthy people as well as great numbers of poor people.

- Availability of foreign exchange

  For a nation to have money for imports requires that nation to be exporting goods. Sometimes imbalances between imports and exports can be overcome by bartering and counter-trading, for example an exchange between nations of imports and exports of the same value. Such an exchange is usually between developed and developing nations, and frequently involves the exchange of raw materials from the developing nation for products from the developed nation. A recent twist on counter-trading is that developing and developed nations are now trading carbon emissions.

Designing and selling products on an international scale can affect the marketing mix in a number of ways, which are summarised in Table 6.

For small companies the challenges posed by international trade may seem huge. However some small companies successfully use the internet to reach a wider international market.

Companies that are seeking global markets tend to go through three distinct stages.

1 *Ethnocentrism*. The home country is seen as being most important and foreign countries as less important, the assumption being that foreign markets are basically the same as the home market.

2 *Polycentrism*. The company identifies differences in markets, adapting products and marketing strategies to local markets and deciding price and promotional strategies locally.

3 *Geocentrism*. The company sees the world as a single market and looks for market segments at a global level to create similar products and marketing strategies on a world scale.

Table 6   Elements of the marketing mix and implications for international markets

Element	Considerations for international markets
Product	cultural, climatic, technical and economic issues may affect product design; products will need to be modified for different power supplies and consumer preferences, for example European households prefer front-loading washing machines, North American households prefer top loaders
Price	pricing has to be done within the currency and income levels of the target market – this can lead to problems when exchange rates fluctuate
Place	distribution systems vary from nation to nation – some nations like to purchase by mail order or through the internet, others buy large quantities of goods in hypermarkets
Promotion	cultural differences make it difficult to create a promotional campaign that can be used globally
People	local staff employed in target markets may have a different cultural understanding of the company and the product
Processes	if a company tries to replicate purchasing processes appropriate to the host country in other countries that do not share the same cultural understanding, this may inhibit sales in those countries and create a barrier to diffusion
Physical evidence	understanding customs and expectations of how purchases are signified is also important for the company image, for example internet purchases may be signified by an email thanking the customer and confirming the order in their own language, using expressions expected by the culture of that country

It is rarely possible to take a completely global view – even major food and drink manufacturers such as Coca Cola and McDonalds have had to make some local adjustments. However the economic benefits of globalisation perceived by companies drive many towards a geocentric goal.

SAQ 30

How might different views of the global market affect the way products are designed and sold?

8.1.2 Sustainable marketing

In marketing speak, sustainable marketing means building a long-term relationship between the customer and the seller. However companies are beginning to realise that embracing sustainability by taking on board environmental or ethical issues can improve customer perceptions of their brands, stimulate innovation and reduce production costs.

The challenges posed by the development of sustainable products can be great. For example Philips Lighting has developed light-emitting diode lights that can last 60 000 hours, many times longer than even a low-energy lamp. However, if the product is so durable, it rarely needs replacing. How can the company make a profit?

The answer to this may lie in the development of systems, rather than isolated products. Just as Edison worked not just on the original incandescent lamp but also on the electricity supply, it is likely that an integrated approach to products, systems and services will enable companies to develop sustainable products while maintaining financial viability.

The development of services to support sustainable development is discussed by Amory Lovens in his book *Natural Capitalism*. Lovens suggests that in the future, services may be bought, rather than products. He offers the example of a floor-covering service. The supplying company initially lays carpet tiles and then periodically checks them, replacing any that are damaged. The tiles themselves can be recycled and remade so there is little or no waste of materials. Instead of paying for new carpets every so often, the purchaser pays for the service on a regular basis. However, as you will see in later blocks, good ideas such as this do not always succeed.

Different market groups have varying levels of awareness about aspects of sustainability. For environmental issues this can range from the green activist who is aware of the issues, committed to buying green products and concerned for the future, through to complacent or alienated people who see the environment as someone else's problem and would not consider changing familiar brands or paying more for a greener product.

Similar levels of awareness can be identified in relation to ethical issues such as the use of child labour, sweatshops in developing countries and the export of production to countries where there is less environmental legislation.

Many companies are now looking to emerging markets in the developing world as a way of increasing sales and profits. There is an enormous tension between these aims and issues of sustainability. If a large number of people in the developing world become car owners, the resulting pollution would be catastrophic on a global scale – even widespread ownership of electrical goods in these emerging markets could pose problems on an international scale.

Designers can play an important role in reducing the environmental impact of products, but the challenges for the sustainability of the planet need to be addressed by companies, governments and nations. The bottom line is that if the environment is damaged more than it already has been, then the issues of buying and selling products will pale into insignificance. You will read more about how this can be done in the next block.

Key points of Section 8

- Products are designed and made in a global economy, and the sales of products worldwide are affected not only by their intrinsic appeal and marketing but also by the trade between nations.

- Each element of the marketing mix needs to be considered from an international perspective to design appropriate products and strategies.

- Companies seeking global markets can be categorised by three different stances: ethnocentrism, polycentrism, geocentrism. However even global companies frequently have to make local adjustments to appeal to different cultural preferences.

- The challenges of sustainability cannot be ignored. If there is no planet, there are no markets.

9 Markets and the lone inventor

Much of the discussion in this block has been about large business organisations. This may seem to have little to do with the individual inventor who has a good idea they think will sell. However there are some fundamental lessons here that apply equally well to a large design team or to a lone inventor.

9.1 Finding out about the market

Some inventors get carried away with the technical aspects of their invention and forget to think about how people will respond and react to it. Anyone who has an idea for a new product should talk to people about their idea – particularly to people who might buy or use it, and people who might sell it. Lone inventors need to establish that their ideas offer relative advantages over existing solutions, and the best way to find this out is by talking to users about their experience of existing products and their opinions of new product ideas.

You have seen a number of user-centred design techniques for finding out how people use and perceive products and what motivates them to choose one product rather than another. Discussing a product topic with a small group of users can identify most of the issues that need to be considered.

However it is important the group is well selected and represents people who could potentially purchase the product. So discussing fishing reels with non-anglers or sewing machines with non-sewers may be of limited value unless you are exploring ideas that might inspire those people to take up these activities.

An inventor who wants to take the step of setting up a company to produce a product will be need to look for niches in the market that are not already catered for. Niche sales can be quite successful when the market is too small for a large company to consider but large enough to support a small company. A lone inventor considering this step needs to identify market niches and then find ways of carrying out qualitative research with potential customers.

Marketing information does not only come from users. Lone inventors need to find and consider information on the size of the market, sales, relevant manufacturing companies, companies making related products and so forth, creating a mini-marketing decision support system to inform their efforts.

Although it may seem contradictory, knowing when to collaborate is important for a lone inventor. For example an inventor who does not have design skills may need to collaborate with someone who understands the types of features that potential buyers might be looking for, or there may be a need to collaborate for some specialist technical help. Further on in the development process the inventor may need to collaborate with a marketing expert to draw up a marketing strategy and devise packaging and promotional materials.

9.1.1 Materials and costings

The lone inventor needs to consider the size of the potential market and the volume of production that is appropriate. This will help to determine the materials and production processes that are most appropriate.

It is imperative that the cost of production is appropriate to the value of the object. If a product is likely to sell in tens of thousands and could be made by injection moulding, this would be a viable production process. However if the product is likely only to sell a few hundred units each year, a less expensive production process may need to be found, which could mean the inventor needs to consider using different materials.

9.1.2 Relative advantage

The lone inventor needs to look critically at their product and find out if other people or companies are offering something similar. If this is the case, the inventor must carefully consider what relative advantages the new product offers. What is its unique selling point? Is it cheaper to make or does it perform better or do something no other product does?

Unless there is some advantage in the new product it may not be worth the cost of taking the idea further. Some say that an idea has to be 10 times better than the competition to win a share of the market. Lone inventors need to evaluate their ideas critically for new products.

In a complex market place with increasingly complex products it is becoming more difficult for an individual to be skilled in everything. Obviously some situations still exist where the individual can have an idea, make the product and market it alone. However such situations are often in areas with a small market where the technology is quite simple.

More frequently there is a need to collaborate at some stage. One approach is to collaborate with a manufacturing company, out-sourcing production of the product to a company with the appropriate facilities. In this situation the lone inventor may take on the role of marketing and distribution. Some large companies have started out in this way. Hewlett-Packard and Apple Computer both started with talented inventors tinkering around creating products in garages. Both companies pride themselves on the innovative free-thinking of the 'garage mentality'.

Exercise 19   Assess the inventions

Consider the products you saw on the video 'Invention now' on the T307 DVD. What were the unique selling points of the products you saw? Had any of the inventors progressed their products through collaboration?

Box 5   Study Buddy

Mary Lyons was an Open University (OU) student who had an idea for a lightweight reading stand that could accommodate OU units and yet be light and portable enough to enable it to be used anywhere. Mary developed a number of prototypes using corrugated plastic to test and refine her idea. As an OU student, Mary focused on the OU market. When the reading stand was ready to be marketed she called it the Study Buddy. She devised a marketing strategy advertising her Study Buddy (Figure 49) in the OU students' newspaper and devising a website to inform potential purchasers.

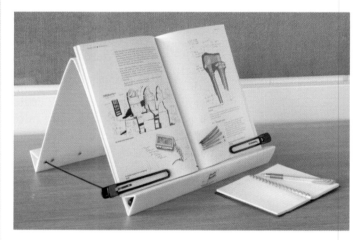

Figure 49   Study Buddy

Initially she fulfilled orders by making the stand herself, but as orders increased she sought out a manufacturer who could produce the stand for her. The stand has undergone a number of iterations and refinements in response to feedback from users, and Mary has diversified her market by gaining the interest of school and health specialists, who could see the usefulness of the reading stand for people with special needs.

Key points of Section 9

Even in the complex markets of today there is still a role for the lone inventor to develop product ideas. However the key lessons are these:

- know and understand your potential markets
- ensure that your idea has a relative advantage over existing products or services and offers a unique selling point
- research existing markets and products
- devise appropriate marketing strategies within your budget and abilities
- bring in expert help where needed.

Answers to self-assessment questions

SAQ 1

What are the three elements common to different definitions of the term market?

The elements are people, goods and services.

SAQ 2

In what ways has the relationship between manufacturer and purchaser or user changed in the past 100 years?

The relationship between manufacturer and purchaser has gone from a production orientation, where the companies sold what they could make, through to a sales orientation, where companies made what they could sell. Emphasis then shifted on to developing product features to make a product appear better than the competition (product orientation). This has become more refined, and manufacturers are now seeking to identify customer needs (consumer orientation), build customer loyalty (relationship or brand marketing) and meet cultural concerns (societal and ethical marketing).

SAQ 3

Three levels at which companies need to consider markets are discussed in 'Importance of markets'. How do these map onto the innovation spiral?

The three levels could be mapped on to the innovation spiral in Figure 8 as follows.

- Strategic planning is carried out from the idea stage at the inner part of the spiral. However strategic planning goes beyond individual product development to look at potential innovations for the whole company.

- Product development takes place at the development stage.

- Sales and marketing strategies are considered during development and later at the launch stage.

SAQ 4

Explain the terms market diffusion and market saturation.

Market diffusion describes how a product or innovation is adopted by the market – as more and more people buy the product it is more widely diffused. At the point when the majority of people who are likely to buy the product have done so, the market reaches the point of market saturation.

SAQ 5

What are the four main market sectors? Give an example of each sector.

The main market sectors are:

- consumer, for example domestic appliances

- commercial, for example offices, shops and services industries

- industrial, for example manufacturing companies

- public, for example local government, schools, hospitals, transport.

SAQ 6

What are the links in the distribution chain for consumer goods? How does this differ from the distribution chain for commercial products?

The links in the distribution chain for consumer goods may be from manufacturer to wholesaler to retailer to consumer, although for goods purchased at super-retailers a wholesaler may not be involved. For commercial products the purchasing company is most likely to purchase directly from a wholesaler, although for very large companies and orders purchases may be made directly from the manufacturer.

SAQ 7

What is the role of the wholesaler/agent in the chain of distribution? How might this affect the design of new products?

The wholesaler acts as an intermediary between the manufacturer and the purchaser. Wholesalers need to be convinced of the benefits of a product to enable that product to reach purchasers. Wholesalers can be a source of new product ideas and feedback and may influence designs in this way.

SAQ 8

Identify three possible forms of relationship between manufacturers and purchasers in the product development process.

The three possible forms of relationship are:

- indirect relationships, where there are many links in the distribution chain and no direct contact between manufacturer and purchaser

- commissioning relationships, where the purchaser directly commissions a product

- joint development, where the manufacturer and purchaser work together on the development of new products.

SAQ 9

What is the marketing decision support system and why is it important?

The marketing decision support system (MDSS) essentially is a collection of systems tools and techniques that are used to gather information. This information may be internal such as sales figures, information about the market environment, or information from primary market research. The MDSS is important because it is the system that collects, brings together, interprets and disseminates information about markets to decision-makers within a company.

SAQ 10

Companies collect information on a number of different trends. What are these trends? Can you think of any more examples?

Some of the trends that companies watch are:

- societal trends, demographics, lifestyle, family roles
- economic trends
- government legislation, regulation and standards
- technological trends and scientific advances.

SAQ 11

Draw up a table to show which of the techniques discussed in this section are qualitative and which are quantitative.

Table 7   Qualitative and quantitative techniques

Qualitative	Quantitative
non-directive interviews	postal surveys
semi-structured interviews	structured surveys
focus groups	hall tests
projective techniques	panels
observation	web-assisted telephone interviews
semantic differential scale (can also be quantitative)	internet surveys
	Likert scale
	point-of-sale information, retail audits, electronic panels

SAQ 12

Which techniques are most useful for finding out about established products and planning incremental innovations?

Any of the techniques could be used for finding out about established products and incremental innovations. The techniques chosen will depend upon what the researcher wants to find out about user preferences, needs and perceptions. Quantitative techniques are frequently used to plan incremental innovations, but, increasingly, focus groups, observation and interviews are also used to inform the planning process.

SAQ 13

Which techniques are most useful for planning and testing radically new products and technical innovations?

For radically new products qualitative techniques are useful because they offer an insight into the perceptions and motivations of potential purchasers that can inform the new product development process.

SAQ 14

What are the original 4 Ps of the marketing mix? Briefly explain their significance for designers.

Product

The designer needs to create a product that works, is reliable and has attractive features. They may also have to consider compatibility and standards.

Price

The designer needs to design a product that offers value for money, for a production cost that is acceptable to the manufacturer.

Place

The designer needs to design a product that appeals to the geographical market, and that can be packed efficiently and at a location where components are sourced from reliable suppliers.

Promotion

The designer needs to design a product that communicates to purchasers through the way it looks.

SAQ 15

What are the new Ps of the marketing mix? Briefly explain their significance for designers.

Process
The designer may need to be aware of the purchasing process.

Physical evidence
The designer may need to design icons to show that a user has purchased a digital service.

Properties
The designer needs to design the aesthetics of a product and also other properties such as environmental qualities.

People
The designer may need to be aware of the people who will act as intermediaries in the selling of a product, and may have to take their needs and concerns into account.

Pleasure
If a designer can design a product that is pleasurable to use, the product will have added value, which will make it more desirable to potential purchasers.

SAQ 16

Identify three ways standards affect the design of products.

- Government standards set out technical expectations for safety and quality.

- Standardisation of components requires designers to consider the interchangeability of components, whether bought in or designed in-house.

● Industry standards affect the design of products for which new formats and dominant designs emerge and compatibility has to be considered.

SAQ 17

Draw a diagram of the product life cycle and show where the five categories of purchasers described above make their purchases.

See Figure 50.

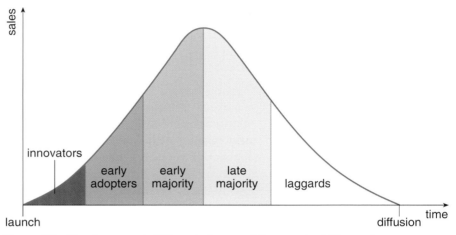

Figure 50   Purchasers at different stages of the product life cycle
Source: adapted from Rogers (2003)

SAQ 18

What pricing strategies might be adopted at different stages of the product life cycle?

At the launch and growth stages, when costs are high, the price may also be high. At the maturity stage, as costs fall because of increasing sales or improvements to the production process, the price may fall. This strategy is designed to encourage more people to buy the product. In the decline phase, prices are likely to be reduced to compete with other companies in the market or shift existing stock. However this all depends upon the overall pricing strategy adopted by the company, and whether this is one of rapid or slow skimming or rapid or slow penetration. A company aiming for rapid penetration of the market may set prices low and accept little profit in the early stages of the product cycle, so that the product gains market dominance.

SAQ 19

What advantages does a user-centred approach to design have over conventional market research techniques?

With user-centred design the designers have a greater understanding of users, their experiences and their needs, from the start of the design process. This understanding brings new insights and ideas market research alone may not identify.

SAQ 20

How can the results of user-centred research be brought into the design process?

The results of user-centred research are frequently brought into workshops, where the whole design team can engage with it. Designers favour visual communication as a way to present this research. Developing personas, fictional characters with the user characteristics, enables the designers to create scenarios for the future use of the product.

SAQ 21

What is the role of the testing house in the product design and development process?

Testing houses are used in several ways. Scientific laboratory tests to examine performance, functions and safety are commissioned by manufacturers requiring independent testing, both to meet regulations and to inform the consumer. Energy testing is carried out to meet legislative requirements. Consumer tests of various kinds are also performed to test user reactions to products at an advanced stage of product development.

SAQ 22

How has the focus of design evolved over the past 100 years?

Over the past 100 years the focus of design has shifted from the *function* of products to the creation of *value-added* features and has now moved on to the design of the *user experience*.

SAQ 23

How have companies sought to expand markets?

Companies have sought to expand markets by both technological and geographical expansion. Technological expansion means investing in the development of technologies, such as information and communications technologies, which enable the creation of new generations of products. Geographical expansion means seeking out new markets in different parts of the world.

SAQ 24

What is experience design?

Experience design looks at the total experience of the user from the first contact with the product onward. It places the user at the centre of the design of new products. The term is used to describe the techniques and processes of design used by Philips Design and described in the article in Exercise 17 in Section 5.

SAQ 25

What is the total product concept?

The total product concept says that products can be viewed at three levels: the core product, the actual product and the total product. For example the core product of a mobile phone is the services it offers, such as telephoning and video messaging. The actual product refers to the aspects that affect user perceptions of the product, including styling, brand, packaging and consumer knowledge of the product. The total product includes such factors as the purchasing process, contracts, warranties, insurance, repairs and servicing.

SAQ 26

What factors influence perceptions of the actual (or formal) product?

Factors such as reliability and ease of use, as well as value-added features and aesthetics, will affect perceptions of the actual product.

SAQ 27

Name three factors that may influence the total (or augmented) product.

Factors such as delivery times, ease of installation and maintenance will affect perceptions of the total product.

SAQ 28

Why is it helpful for designers to know about perceptions and cultures?

It is helpful for designers to know about perceptions and cultures because this can help them better to understand the users and market groups they are designing for. Understanding what motivates people to buy products, and having some knowledge of cultural beliefs, can help designers to design products that have appeal and appropriate cultural meanings.

SAQ 29

What influences purchasing decisions in an industrial setting?

Purchasing decisions in an industrial setting are influenced by perceptions and motivations, just as are consumer purchases. However the purchasing decision will also be influenced by the demands of the organisation and the relationships with suppliers. The decision will also be influenced by the nature of the product, whether raw material, fabricating material or parts, installations, accessory equipment or operating supplies.

SAQ 30

How might different views of the global market affect the way products are designed and sold?

The design and sale of products will be affected by the view the company adopts, whether it is ethnocentric, polycentric or geocentric. Ethonocentric companies will manufacture products that meet the perceived needs of the home market. Polycentric companies will identify market differences and adapt strategies to local markets. Geocentric companies will look for global market segments and may make little or no adjustment to products to meet local needs and cultures.

References and further reading

Aarts, E. H. L. and Marzano, S. (2003) *The New Everyday: Views on Ambient Intelligence*, Rotterdam, 010 Publishers.

Arhippainen, L. (undated) *Capturing User Experience for Product Design* [online], University of Oulu. Available from: www.vtt.fi/virtual/adamos/material/arhippa2.pdf (accessed 19 December 2005)

Assael, H. (1990) *Marketing Principles and Strategy*, Chicago, Dryden Press.

Attfield, J. and Kirkham, P. (eds) (1989) *A View from the Interior*, London, Women's Press.

Barthes, R. (1972) *Mythologies*, London, Jonathan Cape.

Bevelo, M. and Brand, R. (2003) 'Brand design for the long term', *Design Management Journal*, vol. 14, no. 1, pp. 33–39. Also available online at www.dmi.org (accessed 19 December 2005).

Beynon, M., Curry, B. and Morgan, P. (2001) 'Knowledge discovery in marketing: an approach through rough set theory', *European Journal of Marketing*, vol. 35, no. 7–8, pp. 915–937, MCB University Press. Also available online at www.ingentaconnect.com (accessed 19 December 2005).

Black, A. (undated) *User-centred Design* [online], Design Council. Available from: www.design-council.org.uk (accessed 1 August 2005).

Blythe, M. et al (2003) 'Gathering requirements for inclusive design', in Gunter, K., Smith, A and French T. (eds), *Proceedings of 2nd BCS HCI Workshop on Culture and HCI: Bridging Cultural and Digital Divides*, University of Greenwich. Also available online at www.smartthinking.ukideas.com (accessed 19 December 2005).

Carrier, J. (1995) *Gifts and Commodities*, London, Routledge.

Chisnall, P. (1994) *Consumer Behaviour* (3rd edn), Maidenhead, McGraw Hill.

Crouch, S. (1984) *Marketing Research for Managers*, London, Heinemann.

Datshefski, E. (2001) *The Total Beauty of Sustainable Products*, Hove, England, RotoVision.

Design Council, (undated) [online], Design Council. Available from: www.design-council.org.uk (accessed 2004).

Fiell, C. and Fiell, P. (2000) *Industrial Design A-Z*, Köln, Taschen.

Fiell, C. and Fiell, P. (2001) *Designing the 21st Century*, Köln, Taschen.

Forty, A. (1986), *Objects of Desire*, London, Thames and Hudson.

Gaver, W. (1996) 'Affordances for interaction: the social is material for design', *Ecological Psychology*, vol. 8, no. 2, pp. 111–29.

Hawn, C. (2004) 'If he's so smart ... Steve Jobs, Apple, and the limits of innovation', *Fast Company*, issue 78, January 2004. Also available online www.fastcompany.com/magazine/78 (accessed 19 December 2005).

Jackson, P. (2000) *Commercial Cultures: Economies, Practices, Spaces*, Oxford, Berg.

Kotler, P. (1988) *Marketing Management*, Upper Saddle River, NJ, Prentice Hall.

Kran, B. (2004) *Promoting Prius in US*, Cranfield, European Case Clearing House.

Le Compte, M.D. and Schensul, J.J. (1999) *Designing and Conducting Ethnographic Research*, Walnut Creek, CA, AltaMira Press.

Lee, N. and Munro, R. (2001) *The Consumption of Mass*, Oxford, Blackwell.

Leonard, D. and Rayport, J.F. (1997) 'Spark innovation through empathic design', *Harvard Business Review*, vol. 75, no. 6, pp. 102–13.

Levitt, T. (1986) *The Marketing Imagination*, New York, The Free Press.

Mackay, H. (ed) (1997) *Consumption and Everyday Life*, London, Sage.

Marzano, S. (1998) *Creating Value by Design*, London, Lund Humphries.

Mazanec, J. (2001) 'Neural market structure analysis: novel topology-sensitive methodology', *European Journal of Marketing*, vol. 35, no. 7–8, pp. 894–916. Also available online at www.ingentaconnect.com (accessed 19 December 2005).

Mitchell, A. (2001) *Right Side Up: Building Brands in the Age of the Organised Consumer*, London, Harper Collins.

Myerson, J. (2001) *IDEO: Masters of Innovation*, London, Laurence King.

Papanek, V. (1991) *Design for the Real World*, London, Thames and Hudson.

Norman, D. (1999) 'Affordance, conventions and design', *Interactions*, vol. 6, no. 3, pp. 38–43.

Open University (1996) T302 *Innovation: design, environment and strategy*, Block 3, 'Markets and innovation', Milton Keynes, The Open University.

Philips (1996) *Vision of the Future*, Eindhoven, Philips Design/V+K Publishing.

Philips Design (2002) 'The evolving roles of technology and design' [online]. Available from www.design.philips.com (accessed 1 August 2005).

Rogers, E.M. (2003) *Diffusion of Innovations* (5th edn), London, Simon & Schuster.

Von Stamm, B. (2003) *Marketing Innovation Design and Creativity*, Chichester, John Wiley.

Swift, J. (1994) *Gulliver's Travels*, London, Penguin Books.

Woodham, J. (1983) *The Industrial Designer and the Public*, London, Pembridge Press.

Acknowledgements

Grateful acknowledgement is made to the following sources for permission to reproduce material within this book.

Every effort has been made to contact copyright holders. If any have been inadvertently overlooked the publishers will be pleased to make the necessary arrangements at the first opportunity.

Text

Exercise 16: article courtesy of The Design Centre, from www.design-council.org.uk/usercentreddesign

Tables

Table 9.1: reproduced by permission of John Wiley & Sons Limited. Tables 9.2, 9.3 and 9.4: reproduced by permission of Blackwell Publishing. Table 9.5: reprinted by permission of Harvard Business Review. From 'Spark innovation through emphatic design' by Leonard, D. and Rayport, J.F., November–December 1997 © 1997 by the Harvard Business School Publishing Corporation; all rights reserved.

Figures

Figure 2: courtesy of Chetwood Associates. Figure 3: taken from www.amazon.co.uk. Figure 4: courtesy of The Body Shop. Figure 5: courtesy of Philips. Figures 7a and b: Getty Images. Figure 7c: courtesy of Apple Computer Inc. Figures 10a and 10b: courtesy of Panasonic UK Ltd. Figure 11: courtesy of 3M Health Care. Figure 13 a and b: by permission of Haldo Developments Limited. Figure 14: courtesy of Philips. Figure 15: by permission of the Ford Motor Company Limited. Figure 16: adapted from Kotler, P., *Marketing Management* (1988), Pearson Education. Figure 17: © Julian Brown. Figure 18: adapted from Kotler, P., *Marketing Management* (1988), Pearson Education. Figure 20: Helen Hamlyn Research Centre. Figure 21: courtesy of Direction Consultants. Figure 22: Getty Images. Figure 23: taken from www.harrispollonline.co.uk. Figure 27: courtesy of Philips. Figure 29: courtesy of Tom Parker. Figure 30: © yell.com. Figure 35: Science and Society Picture Library. Figures 37 a b and c: © ACM. Figure 38: Helen Hamlyn Research Centre. Figure 39: Helen Hamlyn Research Centre. Figures 40 a, b, c, d and e: courtesy of Philips. Figure 43: courtesy of Toyota Manufacturing (UK) Ltd. Figures 44 a and b: courtesy of Volkswagen UK. Figure 45: taken from www.apple.com. Figure 46: courtesy of Phillips. Figure 47: courtesy of Philips. Figure 50: adapted from Rogers, E.M., *Diffusions of Innovations*, 2003, Simon & Schuster.